GET MORE OUT OF YOUR MARCO POLO GUIDE

IT'S AS SIMPLE AS THIS

1 go.marco-polo.com/lkd

2 download and discover

GO!

WORKS OFFLINE!

SYMBOLS

INSIDER TIP Insider Tip

★ Highlight

●●●● Best of ...

☼ Scenic view

♥ Responsible travel: fair
trade principles and the
environment respected

(*) Telephone numbers
that are not toll-free

**PRICE CATEGORIES
HOTELS**

Expensive over £200
Moderate £120–200
Budget under £120

Prices are per night for a
double room with breakfast

**PRICE CATEGORIES
RESTAURANTS**

Expensive over £20
Moderate £10–20
Budget under £10

Prices are for a typical
meal at that establishment
without drinks

CONTENTS

MAPS IN THE GUIDEBOOK
(120 A1)) Page numbers and coordinates refer to the road atlas
(0) Site/address located off the map
Coordinates are also given for places that are not marked on the road atlas
(U A1) Coordinates for the street maps of Bowness, Gras-mere, Kendal and Keswick on the inside back cover

(*A–B 2–3*) refers to the removable pull-out map
(*a–b 2–3*) refers to the additional inset map on the pull-out map

INSIDE FRONT COVER:
The best highlights

INSIDE BACK COVER:
Street maps of Bowness, Grasmere, Kendal and Keswick

The best MARCO POLO Insider Tips

Our top 15 Insider Tips

INSIDER TIP **Cheers, Coniston!**

More than just a pub: the *Black Bull Inn* in the village of Coniston also brews its own ale – which is excellent with the good food that is served here (photo above) → p. 52

INSIDER TIP **Tea time**

At the *Inn on the Lake* (photo on right) you have wonderful views of Ullswater – and can also enjoy afternoon tea with scones and clotted cream → p. 86

INSIDER TIP **Stay with a star chef**

L'Enclume in Cartmel is the only Michelin two-star restaurant in the Lake District. It is also a lovely place to stay → p. 42

INSIDER TIP **Welcome the winter**

A little light in the dark season: every year in November, the *Holker Estate* holds its Winter Market with lots of food and crafts. A nice little taster for Christmas → p. 109

INSIDER TIP **Food, glorious food**

All the specialities of the Lake District in one shop: *James and John Graham* in Penrith sell everything the region produces, from cheese to gin → p. 79

INSIDER TIP **Ice, ice, baby!**

Whether clotted cream or blueberry: the creamy milk produced by Jersey cows gives the ice cream made at *Abbott Lodge* near Lowther its creamy flavour → p. 82

INSIDER TIP **Stop at the farm shop**

Sizergh Castle has a lot to offer. Don't miss the *Farm Shop* nearby where you can also get a cup of coffee → p. 49

INSIDER TIP **Hostel with views**

On Honister Pass you will find a *youth hostel* that is one of the most impressive in England – well, at least as far as the views are concerned, which stretch right down into the valley → p. 63

INSIDER TIP Railway and Co-operative Heritage

In the mood for a touch of life in the city? Although the *Furness Railway* is no longer a railway, the name now applies to a pub with boutique hotel rooms in Barrow-in-Furness. So although you're in the middle of the town, you're not quite in all the hustle and bustle → p. 59

INSIDER TIP Boat ride to Brantwood

Brantwood, formerly the home of the writer John Ruskin, is a popular destination. It's best to come by *boat from Coniston,* because the trip across the lake is an experience in itself → p. 53

INSIDER TIP Quiz time!

How about a general knowledge quiz? At *The Farmers* in Ulverston, every Thursday there is a pub quiz with lots of questions on current and historical events. It's great fun even if you don't win → p. 58

INSIDER TIP Living with history

The National Trust runs a lot of the most popular attractions in the Lake District, and also rents out *rooms and holiday apartments,* all housed in lovely old buildings → p. 112

INSIDER TIP Lakes on the Rock

At the *Kendal Calling Festival* every summer, high-calibre rock and pop bands perform at Lowther Deer Park → p. 108

INSIDER TIP Have alpaca, will travel

Have you ever taken an alpaca for a walk? You can on the *Lingholm Estate* on Derwent Water – they are calm and sociable → p. 106

INSIDER TIP A clean thing

The soaps produced by the *Soap Company* in Keswick make lovely gifts. They are available in lots of fragrances from Borrowdale Apple to Watermelon → p. 68

BEST OF ...

GREAT PLACES FOR FREE
Discover new places and save money

FOR FREE

● *Guided walks through the National Park*
Guided tours can be expensive, however the National Park Authority occasionally offers tours free of charge → p. 102

● *Into the cathedral for free*
Many of the cathedrals in England charge an admission fee, but not in *Carlisle:* here you can still visit free of charge. (photo) → p. 80

● *Experience the atmosphere of the turf*
Horse races in Cartmel are an institution, but they're also expensive. If you don't want to bet, save the entrance fee! The trick: don't park your car at the main car park, but go to the end of the race track – there's no charge for watching the events, and parking is free as well → p. 41

● *No charge for the Bridge House*
In some cases, admission fees for attractions in the Lake District have rocketed. There is very little that you won't have to dig into your pocket for. However, there is still no charge for visiting one of the most unusual buildings: *Bridge House* in Ambleside → p. 34

● *Houses with history*
Listed buildings are big in Great Britain, and the admission charges for visiting them are often high. However, every year for a whole weekend in September you can visit them for free on the *Heritage Open Days* → p. 112

● *A museum for free*
The *Dock Museum* in Barrow-in-Furness still doesn't charge visitors – unlike almost every other museum in the Lake District. Experience the exciting maritime past of this underestimated treasure! → p. 58

●●●● Dots in guidebook refer to "Best of" tips

● *What a lovely day!*
What could be more relaxing than winding down at the end of the day with a pint of beer? Visit a pub in one of the small towns or villages, and get chatting to the locals at the bar – perhaps at the *Hole in t'Wall* in Bowness → p. 39

● *Get your hiking boots on*
Whether you're particularly sporty or not, a walk in the area, long or short, is an essential part of any visit to the Lake District. The route from Grasmere to little *Easedale Tarn* (photo) is a bit steep, but it's manageable → p. 45

● *On the tracks with "Ratty"*
Great Britain used to be the land of the railway, but many of the smaller routes in particular have been closed down. But at least one of them has survived as a museum railway: the *Ravenglass and Eskdale Railway,* "Ratty" for short, which runs from Ravenglass to the foot of England's highest mountains → p. 54

● *Up the pass*
Mountain passes can cause car drivers to break out in a sweat – but you are rewarded with sensational views. *Kirkstone Pass* between Ambleside and Lake Ullswater is one of the loveliest. Treat yourself to a break at the Kirkstone Inn when you get to the top → p. 86

● *Paddling on the lake*
It's obvious how the Lake District got its name, and where better to experience it than on a *little boat trip?* Hire a boat and paddle along the shore, for instance in Windermere → p. 102

● *Alone with the sheep*
There are tens of thousands of Herdwick sheep in the Lake District, and sooner or later you will encounter these woolly fur-legged fellows – most certainly on a walk around *Lake Buttermere* → p. 61

ONLY IN

BEST OF ...

● *History on four wheels*
The *Lakeland Motor Museum* contains hundreds of classic cars and motorbikes from all over the world. You don't have to be a car enthusiast to appreciate these old beauties → p. 40

● *A drop of the hard stuff*
Gin and whisky: the production process can be so gripping that you forget all about the weather – at least during the subsequent tasting in the *Lakes Distillery* on Bassenthwaite Lake. Best leave the car behind → p. 69

● *My home is my castle*
The Lake District is full of history! Use a rainy day to visit one of the many castles or country estates and learn a lot about the history of the people who live there. One exciting option is *Sizergh Castle* near Kendal → p. 49

● *Shop till you drop*
Grab your umbrella and head off for some shopping in one of the small towns in the Lake District – such as Keswick. You'll stay dry in the shops, and you might even be able to pick up a bargain or two → p. 68

● *Curtain up*
Of course, everyone wants to be outside in the Lake District – but if it rains, just stay in the dry and treat yourself to a performance at the *Theatre by the Lake* in Keswick → p. 64

● *Into the water!*
If you're going to get wet, then get really wet: at the *Penrith Leisure Centre,* which has several diving platforms, a fitness studio and even badminton courts waiting for you → p. 107

RAIN

RELAX AND CHILL OUT
Take it easy and spoil yourself

● *Relaxing on the lake*
Relax on the deck of a pleasure boat on one of the lakes, enjoy the peace and do – well, absolutely nothing. One lovely ride, for instance, is on the *Steam Yacht Gondola* on Coniston Water → **p. 51**

● *Pampering in the spa*
No matter how active you are with walking and other activities, at some point the day will come when there's one thing you really must do: spend some time at a spa. In the Lake District, they are mainly in the hotels such as *Another Place* on Ullswater → **p. 86**

● *Tea overlooking the village*
The *cream tea* is a British institution. There's probably nowhere nicer to enjoy one than in a fabulous café in a tiny village – like *Baldry's Tea Room* in Grasmere → **p. 44**

● *Deep breathing in the garden*
Get a good book and a cuppa, and fall into one of the deck chairs outside *Allan Bank* in Grasmere. Enjoy the views of the lake, breathe in ... and relax (photo) → **p. 44**

● *Bon appetit!*
Treat yourself to some fine dining – for example at the *Castle Dairy* in Kendal → **p. 47**

● *Time-out at a hotel*
Even though it might cost a few pounds, treat yourself to a stay in a hotel. Book one with large, beautiful rooms and lots of lounges where you can read, doze and be waited on. Perfect: *The Belsfield* in Bowness → **p. 39**

INTRODUCTION

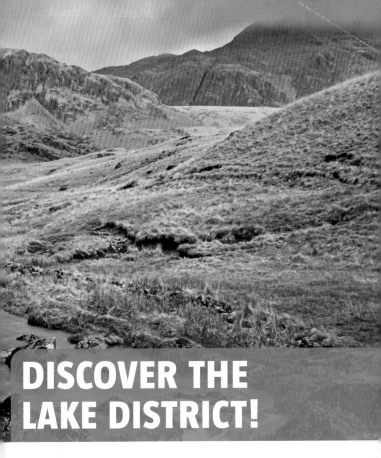

DISCOVER THE LAKE DISTRICT!

The Lake District, the *district of the lakes*. What an understatement! Of course, there are lakes here in the north west of England – including some of the loveliest in the UK, and Windermere is the biggest one in the country. And more importantly: *there are mountains*. And what mountains! All of the elevations in England of more than 914 m/3,000 ft are in the Lake District, which is in the county of Cumbria. Steep mountain passes wind their way up them. At the top, expect the views to take your breath away. Especially on clear days, what nature has created over millions of years is *beautiful enough to move you to tears*.

At 978 m/3,208 ft, the highest peak is Scafell Pike in the north west. Only Scotland and Wales have higher mountains. Because the people here know that they are lucky enough to live in *one of the most stunning places in the British Isles*. The poet William Wordsworth described the Lake District as "the loveliest spot that man hath ever found". He should know: Wordsworth grew up in Cockermouth on the outskirts of what is now the National Park, and spent by far the greater part of his life there, in Grasmere and Rydal. With their ceaseless enthusiasm for the area, he and other writers unintentionally laid the roots for mass tourism.

Photo: Eskdale

Just let go: time isn't particularly important on Derwent Water

The *Lakes,* as the Lake District is called around here, measures 912 mi², which is approximately the same size as Dorset in South West England. The *National Park* was established in 1951, one of a total of 15 in the UK, and in 2017 it was designated a Unesco World Heritage Site. In its decision the Unesco committee praised the area's beauty, the farming and the inspiration the Lake District had provided to several artists and writers. A long-held dream came true for the people of Cumbria: They have been trying to get World Heritage status since 1986. In 2017 the National Park became the 31st place in the UK on the list. It is now mentioned alongside Stonehenge, Bath and several other important places in the country.

But even before tourist numbers rose from 15.8 million in 2009 to 19.2 million in 2017, the Lake District has long been a top holiday hotspot, especially for UK

500 million years BC
Most of the mountains in the Lake District are formed, based on earlier volcanic eruptions

11,000 BC
Trough valleys formed in the last Ice Age that now contain most of the lakes in the Lake District

3000 BC
The first people settle in the Lake District. They form many of the stone circles

43 AD
After two unsuccessful campaigns, the Romans conquer Britain

120 AD
Hadrian's Wall was built as a fortification between

visitors. They are spending a total of £ 1.2 billion each year and provide about 18,000 jobs in the area.

Since becoming a World Heritage Site, the Lake District attracts even more visitors from around the globe. This is probably the main reason for several proposals for new tourist attractions. Plans for a zip

Relaxing in centuries-old villages

wire have been discussed in earnest as well as proposals for a cable car near Keswick were floated. There is even a new way of getting to the National Park: Carlisle Lake District Airport will open in spring 2019 for commercial passenger flights. Belfast, Dublin and Southend are on the list as first destinations. Although the airport is not

the coasts at Carlisle and Newcastle. The Romans wanted it as protection against the Scots, whose land they were unable to conquer

13th century
Coal mining starts

1778
"A Guide to the Lakes" by Thomas West is published. The book marks the start of tourism in the Lake District

1847
The railway age comes to the Lake District with the Kendal and Windermere Railway. Over the following years, the traffic network is extended to include steamships on all the major lakes

based inside the National Park but north of Carlisle, it will be an easier way to get here, especially for a weekend trip. There are also plans to transform Windermere station into the gateway to the Lake District. A lot of things are happening here – but in the end everyone is here mainly for one thing: the landscape.

Lakeland, another name for the district, is dotted with *around 1,000 lakes.* Curiously, though, there is only one proper *lake,* Bassenthwaite Lake: all the others are called *waters* or *meres,* while the very small ones are *tarns.*

At 17 km/10.6 mi, Windermere is one of the longest lakes in England. There is also another record-holder: at 79 m/259.2 ft, Wast Water is the deepest lake in England. However, the people who live there aren't particularly bothered about that: a walk around one of the lakes is a very special kind of relaxation, whether it holds a record or not. When you visit, you will probably have many of the lakes almost to yourself – apart from the *omnipresent Herdwick sheep,* of course. The large, almost too well-developed lakes Windermere and Ullswater are the only places where you will encounter *excursion boats and travel groups from all over the world.* Because word of the beauty of the Lake District has long since spread to Asia and America as well. Some people only want to relax in one of the *centuries-old villages.* There are lots of them, all breathing life into the Lake District. For instance, Grasmere, which is right at the heart of the National Park. In all other respects, though, the National Park focuses on the essential: itself. In fact, a lot of British people only come here for the occasional weekend. Apart from walking, the Lake District is also perfect for climbing, sailing and hang-gliding.

> **Hiking is something of a national sport here**

Hiking is something of a national sport here. There are car parks almost everywhere from where you can set off on a short or long tour. Many of the paths are well developed, although they may be quite steep in places. But that's only to be expected in the mountains. Experienced walkers use the pass hiking routes for a tour, perhaps up Great Gable, along Kirkstone Pass or Hardknott Pass. Those who are perhaps not quite so fit should maybe opt for one of the routes around the lakes. They are usually level, and can easily be walked by anyone.

1951
The Lake District becomes a National Park

1956
Europe's first commercially operated atomic power station is commissioned at Calder Hall. In 1963, Sellafield nuclear plant is built close by

1986
Haig Pit is the last coal mine to close in the Lake District

2015
Storm "Desmond" creates havoc in the Lake District. It was two years before all the damage was put right

2017
The Lake District is made a World Heritage Site

Raising a glass with friends: a typical pub in Ambleside

And there are *more and more sports enthusiasts:* cyclists battle their way up the pass roads to prepare for bigger events, hang-gliders, equestrians. A new generation of hikers is also growing up, and they like exploring sensational landscapes along mostly well developed paths without needing lots of expensive equipment. Minimal risk, maximum fun and a little planning guarantee that there will almost always be a pub at the end.

Maximum fun – and almost always a pub at the end

Best of all: if you find you've had enough of the mountains and lakes, you can head *to the coast* and experience a different side. In the 17th century, wealthy businessmen in the Lake District built ports here in order to take delivery of goods such as spices and rum. Small towns gradually developed around these ports, among them Whitehaven, which have retained the *charm of bygone days* if only in the town centres.

A stark contrast is provided by the hermetically sealed *atomic plant at Sellafield*, well-known throughout the world. As the result of extensive research, the British became one of the leading nuclear powers in the world here, in the west of the Lake District. But it's unlikely that you'll notice anything when you're here, apart from seeing a few signs along the coast. The plant itself is closed off.

17

WHAT'S HOT

1 Drink Pink

New coffee culture You can get a fine espresso almost all over the Lake District! The latest creations are the colourful café lattes, in particular the Pink Latte, a combination of beetroot juice, milk, agave syrup and ginger, and often served with a shot of espresso. You can try it in Kendal at the *Waterside Café (Kent View | www.watersidekendal.co.uk)*, which also serves green matcha latte (green tea, honey and milk) and Golden Tumeric Latte (turmeric, coconut oil, cinnamon and plant milk).

Travelling with flair 2

Around the Lakes in a classic car Hire cars are available everywhere. However, today a lot of people in the Lake District want a driving experience with style, and classic cars are the latest thing. Why drive a Golf or Focus around Borrowdale if you can also do it the typically British way in an old Triumph or Austin Healey? Book through *Lakes and Dales (Midtown Farm | Blencarn | Penrith | tel. 01768 87 90 91 | www.lakesanddales. co.uk/classic-car-hire)*. Be warned, though, that this fun comes with quite a price tag: depending on the car, expect to pay from £175 upwards – unlimited mileage included.

3 The gin of life

With a shot Have you ever tried gin yoghurt? Gin ice cream? Salmon with a touch of gin? A dash of the bitter stuff adds a very special flavour to everything. Gin-o-mania is widespread in the supermarkets of the Lake District. The *Sainsbury's* in Penrith is particularly well equipped. And if you'd rather stick to the original: distilleries such as the Lakes Distillery and Bedrock make very fine gins. You can try them in almost any pub in the National Park.

Boarding on the mountains

Off on your board Want to ride over the hills as if you were on a surfboard on the waves? Skateboards are truly passé in the Lake District – people here use the mountain board. This combination of skateboard and snowboard is fitted with pneumatic tyres that provide a grip almost everywhere – ideal for the conditions in the National Park. Professionals ride them down the mountain, doing leaps and tricks without ever falling on their faces. However, that sort of skill isn't acquired overnight. You can practise mountain boarding almost everywhere in the Lake District – but better wear a helmet and knee protectors, because it's not without its risks. Instruction is provided at *Blaithwaite House (Wigton | tel. 016973 4 23 19 | www.blaithwaite.co.uk).*

Glamping with breakfast

Stylish camping Anyone can stay in a hotel, camping isn't for everyone – but have you ever stayed in an old site trailer? Or in a log cabin? With views of the mountains? Glamping – glamorous camping – has also come to the Lake District. There are lots of little camp sites all over where you will look for tents and caravans in vain. Instead, you stay in comfort with electric lights, often with a wood-burning stove, and breakfast is brought to your door in the morning. Try *Lanefoot Farm (Thornthwaite | tel. 017687 7 80 97 | stayinthornth waite.co.uk)* and at *Park Cliffe (Birks Road | Windermere | tel. 015395 3 13 44 | www.parkcliffe.co.uk).*

IN A NUTSHELL

HISTORY CARVED IN STONE

What on earth are all these stones doing here? Something that has puzzled researchers for centuries: what are the prehistoric legacies in the Lake District and elsewhere in the British Isles? Some of the stones stand 2 m/6.6 ft or more in height, and have obviously been brought here from far away, only to be placed accurately in a circle. Initially people thought it was for religious reasons, but often that was because people couldn't think of anything else. The best-known example in the Lake District is Castlerigg Stone Circle at Keswick. The size of the stones may not be quite as impressive as the more famous Stonehenge in the south of England, but on the other hand it is in a much nicer location – with a view that is almost unmatched. However, there is much of the past to be found under the ground as well as on it. So far, over 16,000 archaeological sites have been uncovered in the Lake District. In the early centuries, the Romans also went right through the Lake District rather than around it. One of their main routes was between Brougham near Penrith and Ambleside, a road now known as the High Street Roman Road. A coastal fort was constructed in Maryport. There was one particular reason for that: the Lake District was not far from Hadrian's Wall, built by the Romans as a fortification against the Scottish enemy.

A life between marmalade and poetry: the Lake District is, in many respects, a special piece of England

A POETIC AREA

How was a person supposed to process the sight of this seamlessly lovely countryside before Facebook, Instagram and the rest had been invented? By writing poetry. And lots of it. William Wordsworth is the best-known writer from the Lake District. He spent almost all of his life here: in Cockermouth, Grasmere and Rydal. The *Lake Poets* were a group of poets who all lived in the Lake District and are considered part of the Romantic Movement. – Because

Wordsworth was already famous in his own lifetime and lived in the Lake District, more and more poets were drawn into his circle. Other areas had painters and their easels; the Lake District had poets with their notebooks. Much of the Romantic Movement in literature was based in the Lake District. And more: it was responsible for tourism even coming to the region. British people all over the country were so fascinated by the glowing admiration expressed by Wordsworth and the rest of the writers for the

Orange and little else: marmalade from the Lake District

countryside that they simply wanted to see it for themselves. An unintended marketing campaign, the success of which has not been beaten to this day.

A PART OF THE WORLD THAT IS WORTH PROTECTING

What do the Great Wall of China, the Statue of Liberty in New York and the Lake District have in common? They are all World Heritage Sites. In 2017, Unesco placed Cumbria's National Park under this special protection that is only given to sites that are unique and appeal for their unique authenticity. The reason given at the time was that the Lake District was an inspiring landscape. Agriculture has been working in harmony with nature for centuries. The area is not only ideal for the Herdwick sheep, but has also produced a whole generation of regional writers. A broad alliance of organisations ranging from the National Trust to the University of Cumbria was involved in the successful nomination. The Lake District is the first British national park to be named a World Heritage Site. The locals hope that it will give the area something of a boost, and not just in tourism. All over the world, the Unesco stamp is seen as a guarantee for very special travel destinations.

ROCK THE LAKES

Sure – everyone comes to see the nature in the Lake District. Everyone? In summer in particular, the festivals and other events attract plenty of visitors, especially "Kendal Calling". This began in 2006 as a relatively low-key event outside Kendal Castle, attracting less than 1,000 participants and bands that hardly anyone had ever heard of. Today this indie meeting has become a major event at Lowther Deer Park. Up to 25,000 people come here every year at the end of July for the four-day rock festival. Bands like the Stereophonics,

Manic Street Preachers and Franz Ferdinand have pulled the crowds in recent years. It's a little more village party-like in August for the Solfest, an indie festival on Tarnside Farm south of Windermere. It began in 2003, also quite small, but now has long been one of the UK's most popular music festivals. The programme is highly varied, ranging from folk to hip-hop, soul to reggae. One rather more traditional festival takes place in May, in Ireby on the northern edge of the Lake District, with a still quite young event of primarily folk music. Many visitors descend on this village with a population of just 160. Also new: Roots 66 in Keswick. When winter has settled in the National Park, The Theatre by the Lake holds a folk festival in February to bring a little life into the cold, dark days.

LET'S GET PHYSICAL

It may look as if two bears are wrestling with each other, but there's no need to be alarmed: Cumbrian Wrestling, also known as Cumberland and Westmorland Wrestling, no longer has anything to do with trench warfare. As far as people know, it is a left-over from the Vikings, and a popular sport at summer fairs – especially at the Grasmere Lakeland Sports and Show, which takes place every year over the August bank holiday. The idea is quite simple: two wrestlers stand on the grass, chest to chest, each with their chin on their opponent's right shoulder and an arm on their back. At the command, they start wrestling; the aim is to get the other contestant off balance and make them fall onto the ground. The second person to fall (or not fall at all) is the winner. A similar version is held in the south of Scotland and a few other northern areas, as well as in some Scandinavian countries.

THE SNOW DISTRICT

Green meadows, purple heather, and everywhere the yellow of the gorse – the Lake District is a riot of colour in summer. But in winter? Often nothing but white. Snow covers the mountain tops as the wind howls through the valleys, and – as all over Europe at this time of the year – there are only a few hours of daylight. Not the time to come? That would be a shame! In winter, the National Park attracts dreamy souls almost as if by magic: loved-up couples who spend hours relaxing in front of the fire, active people who are happy to enjoy a little hike even if the mercury has dropped to a few degrees below freezing. The frosty roofs in many of the villages are perfect for photos, and when the Christmas lights are turned on in December, the romantic setting is perfect. The Lake District isn't quite so well-known with skiers, but that's not to say it can't be done. Helvellyn (950 m/3,117 ft) is known for its snow, and neighbouring Raise (883 m/2,733 ft) even has its own ski club. You can ski down its slopes on an average of 60 days during the season, and depending on the weather there are up to nine runs. But of course, it's not a serious competitor for the Alps, not least because there are no major resorts. If you do want to ski in the Lake District, you'll have to organise everything yourself, including your skis. But there's one big plus: the après-ski in the pub.

THE PLACE FOR MARMALADE

As we all know, the Lake District is well-known for its countryside, but did you know that it is also the centre for orange marmalade? Even though oranges don't even grow here. But the British generally have a preference for it, and Jane Hasell-McCosh, owner of Dalemain Mansion near Penrith, in particular. In 2005, she created an entire festival based on her passion for marmalade. Since then, it has taken place every year in March, and today attracts visitors from all over the world – even Asia is crazy about orange marmalade. In fact, there is now even a marmalade festival in Australia, under license to the Dalemain World's Marmalade Awards.

The burning question is always: which is the best marmalade in the world? In Great Britain, only marmalade made from citrus fruit and in particular from oranges, can be called marmalade. Everything else is *jam.* This has now even been laid down in an EU regulation. At Dalemain in March, everything is about oranges. And not just here: the whole of Penrith is decorated in the colour orange for the festival.

THE DAMPEST PLACE IN ENGLAND

When you come to the Lake District you will unfortunately be coming to the dampest place in Great Britain. On average, 2000 mm of rain fall here every year, and Seathwaite in Borrowdale is the wettest inhabited place in the entire British Isles: it receives around 3552 mm of rain per year. In comparison Essex only receives 500–600 mm of rain per year. Climate change is also becoming increasingly evident in the Lake District, and in 2009 residents had to be airlifted to safety by helicopter after 314.4 mm of rain fell in the National Park in a 24-hour period. The following year, there were serious water shortages in the area as the result of an extreme drought. The weather really does do as it pleases here, which clearly affects countryside, people and animals. Shocked by the flood, the park administration launched the low-carbon Lake District initiative, a comprehensive programme, still in place today, to tack-le climate change in the National Park. Roads are being reinforced, the fresh water situation improved, bridges secured. But take heart: it doesn't always rain in the Lake District, and when it does, then not everywhere, and usually only in quick showers. Anyway, that's why you brought your umbrella.

WHITE VILLAGES, LONG WALLS

You see them everywhere, mainly in the small villages: white houses that are so bright in the sunshine that you'd think you were in southern Europe. But actually, the colour white goes back to a practical tradition. Houses and farmhouses used to be treated with red lead to protect them against the damp. After that they were whitewashed to make them look nicer. Many house-owners still adhere to this colour today, and white houses are a firm fixture in the Lake District. It's a similar story with the numerous stone walls around the fields. They used to mark agricultural areas. It also made sense to build these walls using stones that were turned up when ploughing the fields.

ISLAND OF THE NATION

Grasmere is one of the most tranquil bodies of water in the Lake District, and tiny uninhabited Grasmere Island in it is even more tranquil. Yet history has been written here, and it was an event that permanently changed Great Britain. The then highly-regarded Canon Hardwicke Rawnsley was outraged when this island was offered for sale in 1893. He was absolutely against private land ownership involving mountains, lakes and islands. Together with Sir Robert Hunter and Octavia Hill, at the end of 1893 he made plans for the preservation of significant buildings and lands.

Smile, please: you'll see Herdwick sheep almost everywhere in the Lake District

A little over a year later, the three founded the National Trust. The National Trust's stated aim to is acquire lands and properties, either through purchase or as gifts, so that they can be preserved and enjoyed by everyone. "For ever, for everyone" has been its motto since then. Today, the National Trust owns over 350 buildings, gardens, castles and churches as well as several pubs and entire villages. This amounts to a total of 1.5 percent of the area of Great Britain, including one-quarter of the Lake District and ten percent of the entire British coast. However, the Trust had to wait 124 years for Grasmere, which it only received in 2017.

WHERE THE HERDWICKS LIVE

The children's writer Beatrix Potter gained world fame through her furry little creation, Peter Rabbit – but in fact, her heart belonged to an entirely different animal: Herdwick sheep. This is made most clear in a letter that she wrote to a publisher in 1931. A celebrated championship-winning Herdwick ram with the impressive name of Saddleback Wedgewood had suddenly passed away, she wrote, and the writer – who was already well-known then – made no secret of her sadness. He had been on loan to her at Hill Top Farm, where he had been busy helping to improve her future Herdwick flock. Apparently, it was all too much for him.

Potter's Herdwick sheep are today one of the main landmarks of the Lake District. What makes them so special are their typical grey colour and strikingly friendly faces. Above all, though, they are more suited to the sometimes extreme weather conditions in Cumbria than other breeds. Eventually, Potter did so much for these animals that in the end she owned a total of 17 farms, all of which she left to the National Trust in 1943 – although not without leaving instructions that Herdwick sheep had to be kept there in perpetuity. Almost all of the current world population of Herdwicks lives in the Lake District.

FOOD & DRINK

When you're enjoying a meal in the Lake District, forget the sheep and the slower pace of daily life. Many years ago, there was something of a food revolution in the National Park. In many places, talented chefs have completely transformed the menus of even the smallest pubs and restaurants. Some of them have even had their efforts rewarded with a highly-coveted Michelin star. The frontrunner remains *L'Enclume* in Cartmel, which received two stars a number of years ago.

Never judge a restaurant by its exterior. Even in the most isolated spots, you'll find that the most basic pubs are bursting with culinary excellence. It's better to check that the menu offers more than breakfast and sausages.

There is usually plenty of meat and fish on the menus, and often *locally-grown organic vegetables*, with the occasional cheese from the North of England. The popularity of burgers hasn't missed Cumbria, and for those with a traditional palate, *Cumberland sausages* and *Herdwick lamb*, the meat from the cute local lambs, are among the region's classics.

What is surprising is that the Lake District is a *paradise for vegetarians, vegans and allergy-sufferers*. Although hardly any of the restaurants are entirely meat-free, almost all of them offer vegetarian and vegan dishes in addition to the usual fare. A lot of restaurants also provide gluten, nut and lactose-free meals.

Regional products are the order of the day, and vegetarian food is available everywhere

However, if you're wanting to eat in the National Park, you're not necessarily limited to the restaurants – food festivals have become increasingly popular over the years. In summer, for instance, you can stroll through the *Chilli Festival* in Holker, the *Beer Fest* in Keswick or the *Cumberland Sausage Festival* at Muncaster Castle. And if by chance there's nothing on offer at the time, you can be sure of always finding a culinary sensation in the gourmet village of Cartmel in the south of the Lake District, such as

sticky toffee pudding, which is said to have been invented here.

Thanks to the proximity to Scotland, the selection of whiskies is often surprisingly varied. And like everywhere in England, there is another trendy drink that has never gone out of fashion in the Lake District: *gin*. Even quite basic pubs will often have an excellent selection – including some from the Lake District itself, such as The Lakes, light and smooth in flavour, and Bedrock, a very elegant, complex gin.

LOCAL SPECIALITIES

Cumberland ham – unsmoked ham, rubbed with salt and brown sugar, dry-cured for one month, then washed and dried for another two months

Cumberland sausage – this pork sausage can be up to half a metre long, which is why it is curled into a spiral. It is flavoured with a few herbs and above all pepper; nothing else may be added (photo left)

Damsons – a type of plum which not only grows in the Lake District – but Lyth Valley is well known as one of the best places to grow them because of its micro-climate.

Gingerbread – spices from all over the world were brought into Cumbria's ports. So what makes more sense than to use them for cooking and baking? In Grasmere, this resulted in gingerbread, a type of cake that is as spicy as a helping of curry

Herdwick lamb – due to the weather, these lambs grow more slowly than those in the south of the country. Gourmets claim that makes its meat particularly aromatic

Kendal mint cake – these peppermint blocks are the traditional sustenance for hill-walkers in the Lake District. However, you really have to like the very intensive flavour in order to follow this tradition

Rum butter – butter flavoured with rum, a custom that dates back to the time when rum was imported through Cumbria's ports

Salt marsh lamb – a special kind of lamb that grazes on the coast in the south of Cumbria, and therefore eats lots of seaweed and other plants. This gives the meat a special flavour

Trout – the area is well and widely known for its fresh fish, especially trout from Ullswater

But the standard choice of beverage in any pub is still the pint (0.568 l). Although you'll usually find the same choices on tap as in the rest of the country, there are over *a dozen breweries in the Lake District* alone, including Hawkshead, Keswick Brewing and Jennings. And almost everywhere there will be at least one from the barrel.

Coffee has also become a veritable delight in the Lake District. While the chains such as Costa, Caffè Nero and Starbucks have practically flooded the UK with their wide range of espresso

For the perfect afternoon: Pimm's and lemonade

drinks, in the National Park today almost every pub has an expensive machine to make its flat whites & co. Look for the little independent cafés in towns such as Grasmere and Windermere, where you'll find *genuine Italian barista-style coffees*, often accompanied by home-made cakes. INSIDER TIP Some small companies even roast coffee locally, such as the Red Bank Coffee Roasters in Coniston, who have several excellent varieties on offer.

The coffee is best served with beautiful homemade cakes. When in the Lake District, don't make do with the standard supermarket cakes; almost every town and village still has local bakeries and cafés that fire up their ovens early in the morning for that day's produce. And if you'd like to try your hand at making your own, in recent years *cookery schools* have opened in several places and offer one-off evening classes for visitors.

Markets usually take place at the weekend, and the local Booths supermarkets also offer *local products* and are an excellent source of culinary delights if you want to take a picnic with you on your walk. You'll also find healthy snacks. They might not have a star, but the best thing you can do here doesn't require any particular culinary skills: enjoying the views of one of the mountains or lakes will turn even the humblest snack into the perfect picnic.

SHOPPING

You certainly shouldn't have any difficulties finding gifts in the Lake District: There are lovely items in every town and village, at every tourist attraction, and occasionally even in the middle of the countryside. If you're a lover of department stores and big fashion boutiques, though, expect to be disappointed. At best, you'll find them in Carlisle or other big towns in the National Park.

ANTIQUES

You will find at least one antiques shop in every big town, such as Kendal, Keswick or Cartmel. Especially popular are old photographs, porcelain and glasses, but there are also large items of furniture, whisky barrels and sometimes even a genuine British letterbox.

COOKING

One of the biggest British names for kitchen utensils hails from the *Lake District: Lakeland* (formerly Lakeland Plastics) has a kind of flagship store in the station of its home town Windermere with a tremendous range of its goods. It rubs off – almost every big town has shops that sell kitchen utensils. Even

the big supermarkets now have their own dedicated departments and they're growing all the time.

FASHION

Look out for small boutiques. The Lake District is particularly good for buying mountaineering and sports clothing. There are many specialist shops, which helps to keep prices reasonable. *Horsley* and *Lakeland Skirts* are manufacturers in Kendal who produce ladies' fashions in the modern country-house style. There are also lots of factory outlet stores of the sports brand *New Balance* all over the National Park, which is due to the fact that the company has a factory near Maryport. *Chapman* is a company in Carlisle that produces high-quality bags.

FOODS

The Lake District produces many fresh foods, such as fish, meat and dairy products, although they are not really suitable for taking home as gifts. However, the area is also known for its cheeses, and Cheddar is the main variety produced in Cumbria (its geographic name is not protected). You'll

You don't need the big fashion labels in the Lake District – you'll be filling your suitcase with little accessories

find an excellent selection of Cumbrian cheeses in special shops in Keswick, Cartmel and Penrith. Gin, vodka and whisky have a better shelf-life, as do cider and beer from the Lake District (available from all big supermarkets). One classic is spicy *gingerbread* from Grasmere.

GARDEN CENTRES

What would Great Britain be without its gardens? Certainly nowhere near as colourful. A lot of the plants that are typical of the Lake District can be purchased at the large garden centres that have sprung up all over the country. They also sell all kinds of pots and decorations for the garden. Typical plants in England are roses, hydrangeas, rhododendrons and lavender.

GIFT ITEMS

Typical souvenirs from the National Park are usually made from materials that are found there: wool, slate or wood. You'll find all kinds of things made from slate, from signs to coasters. Many items are made from Herdwick wool, including cushion covers and bags. Little Peter Rabbit, the hero of the well-known children's "Peter Rabbit" books by Beatrix Potter, is available in many different forms, especially in her own home area of Hawkshead – whether as a stuffed animal, mug or picture. The still fairly new brand INSIDER TIP *Herdy (www. herdy.co.uk)* by contrast is dedicated to the Herdwick sheep in a slightly different way. The cartoon figure is available as egg cups, money boxes, towels and stuffed animals – a very trendy gift.

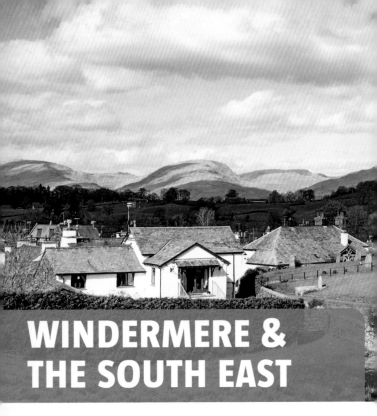

WINDERMERE & THE SOUTH EAST

Everything that is special about the Lake District bundled in one region: in the south east you'll find everything that makes the National Park what it is – idyllic lakes, high mountains, romantic villages, sheep and yet more sheep.

However, this also means that almost every coach stops here. Lots of places are busy, and the popular destinations in particular such as Bowness and Grasmere often seem overrun. If you want to experience the real southeast, it's a good idea to stay overnight. By the time the last day visitors leave in the evening, you will be able to experience the area as it really is. During the day, join the fray and explore the numerous mountains and lakes, such

as tranquil Grasmere or Windermere, the biggest natural lake in England. Whenever you can, you should leave the car at home – there are hiking paths almost everywhere, and for every level of ability. And that's the best way to explore the unique countryside of this region.

Kendal, just outside the Lake District is a proper little town, and effectively the economic centre of the region. All around Windermere are historic buildings such as Wray Castle and Sizergh Castle.

On Sundays in particular, there is nothing better than a boat trip. Simply get aboard a steamer or launcher, sit back, and let your surroundings of mountain scenery, secluded bays and wooded islands work their magic on you.

The tourist centre of the Lake District – with villages, mountains, lakes and much more for which the region is world famous

AMBLESIDE

(126 B1–2) (⌂ E6) Don't be put off: one of the main roads in the Lake District goes right through (pop. 2600), although that seems to make surprisingly little difference to the town with its many Victorian buildings.

Quite the opposite, in fact: due to its location north of Windermere, Ambleside has become a proper little centre of business, envied by other towns in the area. Shops for all occasions define the rather bustling daily life, and there are lots of hotels, pubs and restaurants. A good place for people who start to get twitchy when it gets too quiet in the evenings.

Lake Windermere and its pier is a good kilometre (0.6 mi) from the centre, but that doesn't matter – it means that the crowds of visitors are more evenly spread around. So the best plan is: a stroll, a good look around, and then put your feet up!

Apples were once stored in tiny Bridge House in Ambleside

SIGHTSEEING

ARMITT

Do you like art? Then you will love this little museum, which also has a library and gallery. Founded in 1912, it was supported from the beginning by well-known writers and artists. Beatrix Potter was one of the people who donated works to the Armitt. A relaxing stop, and a change from hiking and boats – especially on a rainy day! *April–Oct Tue–Sat 10am–5pm | admission £5 | Rydal Road | www.armitt.com*

BRIDGE HOUSE ●

This tiny house built on a stone bridge over Stock Beck is one of the most photographed images in the Lake District. It was built in the 17th century as an apple store. Today, two of the rooms in the building display furniture from that time. The slate roof is typical of the era, and the ensemble is completed by the river that flows beneath it. *April–Oct daily 11.30am–4.15pm | admission free | Rydal Road | www.nationaltrust.org.uk/ambleside*

STOCK GHYLL FORCE

Just a short walk east from the centre, this high picturesque waterfall drops 20 m/65.6 ft into a bowl-shaped pool from Stock Beck. The ghyll once powered twelve watermills in Ambleside. None of them are in existence any longer; most have long since been demolished, while others have been converted into residences. Nevertheless, it still gives some impression from the industrial times gone past. *Always open | admission free | 6 Stockghyll Lane*

FOOD & DRINK

COPPER POT CAFÉ ●

A chic little café with street food: burgers, salads and sandwiches are all freshly made using local ingredients. *Church Street | tel. 015394 3 19 11 | www.copperpot.co.uk | Budget*

OLD STAMP HOUSE

The scallops are a dream, and you'll still be in raptures over the haunch of venison the next day. You'll love whatever you order in this first-class restaurant. *Church Street | tel. 015394 3 27 75 | www. oldstamphouse.com | Expensive*

water ski *(£75 per half hour)* and Flyboard *(£55 per half hour)*.

There is a pleasant, easy walk (5 km/ 3.1 mi) west of Ambleside to *Loughrigg Tarn* and on to the little waterfall of *Skelwith Force,* past rivers, another lake, mountains and woods.

LEISURE & SPORTS

Boats are for hire from the pier at Waterhead *(1 hour for £16 | www.wind ermere-lakecruises.co.uk).* This is also where the excursion boats depart on trips to Bowness and Lakeside.

The *Ambleside Climbing Wall (from £8.50 | 101 Lake Road | tel. 015394 3 37 94 | www.amblesideadventure. co.uk)* not only has a small climbing wall just for children, but also organises courses for true pros. At the *Low Wood Bay Resort (Ambleside Road | tel. 015394 3 94 41 | www.englishlakes. co.uk/low-wood-bay/watersports)* about 1.5 km/0.9 mi to the south, you can

WHERE TO STAY

CLAREMONT GUEST HOUSE

Small, unfussy B&B in the centre. The rooms are basic but mostly modern. *6 rooms | Compston Road | tel. 015394 3 34 48 | www.claremontambleside.co.uk | Budget*

WATERHEAD HOTEL ☼

Straight out onto a pleasure boat after breakfast? You can in Ambleside. At this luxurious, traditional hotel on the jetty, you'll enjoy good views and excellent service. *41 rooms | Lake Road | tel. 015394 3 25 66 | www.englishlakes. co.uk | Expensive*

⭐ **Hawkshead**
A village straight out of a film set – idyllic to the last house → p. 36

⭐ **Easedale Tarn**
Little lake with big views: peace and tranquility awaits you here → p. 45

⭐ **Cartmel Racecourse**
Tiny Cartmel becomes a destination for people from all over the country at race time → p. 41

⭐ **Allan Bank**
Let the former home of National Trust co-founder Canon Rawnsley in Grasmere be yours just for a moment → p. 44

⭐ **Lakeside and Haverthwaite Railway**
Ride this old steam train from Windermere to Haverthwaite → p. 40

⭐ **Dove Cottage**
The poet William Wordsworth once lived in this little house in Grasmere. Take a tour and feel as if you've been taken back in time → p. 44

⭐ **Wray Castle**
Actually it is a home, but from the outside it's a neo-Gothic castle – in a most impressive setting → p. 37

MARCO POLO HIGHLIGHTS

INFORMATION

Tourist Information Centre | Central Buildings | Market Cross | tel. 0844 2 25 05 44 | www.amblesideonline.co.uk

WHERE TO GO

HAWKSHEAD ★ (126 B2) (*ω E6–7*)

Peter Rabbit is the symbol of Hawkshead (pop. 500). Almost every shop sells souvenirs of the furry little fellow, yet the medieval village remains intact, and indeed is without equal. Cars must be left in the car park on the outskirts, and it's easy to walk around.

The main attraction is the *Beatrix Potter Gallery (March/April, Sept/Oct daily 10am–4pm, May–Aug 10am–5pm | admission £6.30 | Main Street | www.nationaltrust.org.uk)*, the former office of the writer's husband, which contains many of her paintings and drawings. Potter loved to draw animals most of all, but the rest of the house with its wood floors and uneven walls is just as appealing.

William Wordsworth attended *Hawkshead Grammar School (April–Sept Mon–Sat 10am–1pm and 13.30pm–5pm | admission £2.50 | Main Street | www.hawksheadgrammar.org.uk)* – now a museum, and still furnished exactly as it was in his day. Delicious home-made ice cream is on sale at the INSIDER TIP *Little Ice Cream Shop (Laburnum House | The Square)*. Accommodation in pretty, modernised rooms: *Queen's Head Hotel (13 rooms | Main Street | tel. 015394 3 62 71 | queensheadhawkshead.co.uk | Moderate)* of the 17th century.

HILL TOP (126 B2) (*ω E7*)

West of Windermere is the former home of Beatrix Potter, in a tiny hamlet 12 km/ 7.5 mi south of Ambleside. It still looks as if the writer (who has been dead for many years) has just popped out to do some shopping. The rooms have been restored to the state they would have been in at the beginning of the 20th century. Potter bought the house with the money she made from her first Peter Rabbit book, and it instantly became the source of her inspiration. Hill Top and the surrounding area can be found in her later books. Furniture, books and pictures offer a good insight into the writer's life. The garden contains many local plants and herbs. *March/April, Sept/Oct Sat–Thu 10am–4.30pm, May–Aug daily 10am–5pm | admission £10.40 | Sawrey | www.nationaltrust.org.uk*

LOW BUDGET

Labels at bargain prices: the tiny outlet mall *K Village (1 Riverside Place | Lound Road | www.kvillage.co.uk)* is situated on the banks of the River Kent in Kendal. Although it cannot necessarily be compared with the big shopping centres, it is still worth a visit – not least because parking is cheap in the multistorey car park and you can walk into the town.

Very reasonable evening meals: the *JD Wetherspoon* chain of pubs serves reasonably-priced meals in lovely pubs. Prices for a main course plus an (alcoholic) drink start at £7, and there are almost daily special offers such as curries, steaks or fish & chips. The pub *The Miles Thompson (Allhallows Lane | tel. 01539 81 57 10)* in Kendal is part of the chain.

Weather forecast good, in the mood for a hike? Then get yourself off to Ambleside!

TROUTBECK (126 B2) *(E6)*
A tiny village that is often forgotten: Troutbeck is a little way from the main roads and so small that the post office also sells coffee and cake because hardly anywhere else does. The main attraction is *Townend (May–Oct Wed–Sun 1pm–5pm | admission £6.50 | Holbeck Lane | www.nationaltrust.org.uk/townend)*, a white, 400-year-old farmhouse that has been restored to its original condition both on the outside and on the inside. You'll be greeted by the smell of wood smoke as you walk in; the floorboards creak, and cheery pensioners from the area will happily chat to you about days gone by. The rooms contain furniture from those days, and there are occasional activities, especially for children. British cuisine and a good night's sleep in peace and quiet at the extensively and lovingly refurbished INSIDER TIP *Queens Head Hotel (10 rooms | Town Head | tel. 015394 32404 | www.queensheadtroutbeck.pub | restaurant Expensive, rooms Moderate).*

WRAY CASTLE ★ (126 B2) *(E6)*
You really must see this neo-Gothic castle from the outside. It rises above the shores of Windermere and the countryside beyond, and looks as if at least half the Lake District was once ruled over from here. But it wasn't. Instead, a retired surgeon spent all of his wife's fortune on building the vast estate. Given to the National Trust in 1929, it has only been open to the public for a few years. Inside, cast your eye over the architecture with its lavish wooden decorations and staircases. Having said that, there isn't much more to see – Wray Castle is more or less empty, and with a pool table and toys is aimed more at children. In good weather, treat yourself to some home-made cake and tea from the café and enjoy the fabulous views of the surrounding area from the tables near the main entrance! *April, Nov Sat/Sun 10am–4pm, May–Oct daily 10am–5pm (5.30pm in summer) | admission £9, grounds always accessible at no charge | Ordnance Survey | www.nationaltrust.org.uk*

A lucky move: World of Beatrix Potter in Bowness-on-Windermere

BOWNESS & WINDERMERE

▨▨ **MAP INSIDE BACK COVER**
▨▨ (126 B2) *(𝄞 E7)* **Bowness (pop. 3800) is a charming town on the shores of Windermere which has become something of a tourist stronghold.** Restaurants, hotels and pubs are numerous, but a stroll around Bowness is an obstacle course of selfie sticks and pushchairs. Accommodation here is more expensive than anywhere else in the Lake District. Yet it's still worth visiting for a day – not least for a boat ride on Windermere.

You'll find the exact opposite right next door in Windermere (pop. 2300). A quiet, tranquil town, Windermere has a perfect infrastructure: the small centre has lots of independent shops, the cafés and restaurants are a little more relaxed and of a slightly higher quality than in neighbouring Bowness. The region's biggest supermarket can be found here, and trains stop at the station in Windermere – not in Bowness.

SIGHTSEEING

THE WORLD OF BEATRIX POTTER
(U B5) *(𝄞 b5)*
Beatrix Potter became famous after writing her children's books about Peter Rabbit – books that can still be found on almost every child's bookshelf today. Here you can find famous scenes from the books re-enacted with figurines.

Interesting for children, but otherwise really only for confirmed Peter Rabbit fans. *Daily 10am–4.30pm | admission £7.50 | Crag Brow | Bowness | www.hopskip-jump.com*

FOOD & DRINK

HOLE IN T'WALL ● (U B5) (*ŵ b5*)

At this pub, also known as the New Hall Inn, you can enjoy good food and try a large variety of different of beers from the region. Occasional live music. *Robinson Place | Bowness | tel. 015394 4 34 88 | Moderate*

HOMEGROUND ☺ (0) (*ŵ 0*)

Modern café with fabulous coffee specialities and a small menu based on regional, organic products. *Main Road | Windermere | tel. 015394 4 48 63 | www.homegroundcafe.co.uk | Budget*

PORTO ☺ (U B5) (*ŵ b5*)

Mushroom risotto, monkfish or steak? You may well have had many of the dishes served at this modern restaurant elsewhere – but perhaps not as lavishly presented as here. Delicious British cuisine made with the best local ingredients. *3 Ash Street | Bowness | tel. 015394 4 82 42 | www.porto-restaurant.co.uk | Expensive*

SHOPPING

Most of the shops in Windermere are located between Main Road and Crescent Road. INSIDER TIP *The Northern Line (4 Crescent Road)* has a lovely range of gifts and home furnishings. For a large supermarket with a wide range of regional products, go to *Booths (Victoria Street)* at the station. The shop *Peter Rabbit and Friends* (U B5) (*ŵ b5*) (*Old Midland Bank |*

Bowness) sells all sorts of items related to the story-book bunny.

LEISURE & SPORTS

Rowing and electric boats are ideal for exploring Lake Windermere. You can hire them directly on the jetty in Bowness (U A6) (*ŵ a6*) (*rowing boat £16/hour, electric boats from £26 | Promenade | tel. 015394 4 33 60 | www.windermere-lakecruises.co.uk).* This is also where the excursion boats set out from. Cycling is possible on relatively flat and largely traffic-free paths. Sturdy mountain bikes are available by the day from *Country Lanes Cycle Hire Centre (£24/day | Windermere Railway Station | Station Precinct | tel. 015394 4 45 44 | www.countrylaneslakedistrict.co.uk).*

There is a lovely, short walk from Windermere station to ☆ *Orrest Head.* The hill was the site of the region's first walking trails for tourists. And for a good reason – spoilt as the Lake District is with fabulous views, this is exceptional even by local standards.

WHERE TO STAY

THE BELSFIELD ●
(U B6) (*ŵ b6*)

One of two hotels in England that are furnished by interior design icon Laura Ashley. It is perfectly located right on the jetty, and surrounded by a large garden. Elegant, comfortable – and rather on the expensive side. *62 rooms | Kendal Road | Bowness | tel. 015394 4 24 48 | www.lauraashleyhotels.com/thebelsfield | Expensive*

CRAIGHOLME B&B
(U C4) (*ŵ c4*)

A lovely little B&B in Bowness, but not right on the lake. *3 rooms | 70 Craig*

Walk | tel. 015394 4 83 09 | www.lakes guesthouse.co.uk | Budget

Tourist Information Centre (0) (📖 0) | Victoria Street | Windermere | just down from the station | tel. 015394 4 64 99 | www.windermereinfo.co.uk

WHERE TO GO

BLACKWELL 🎨 (126 B3) (📖 E7)

From the outside, this building 3 km/ 1.9 mi south of Bowness might only look like a lightly coloured, old building, but in fact it is an architectural gem. It was built at the end of the 19th/beginning of the 20th centuries, at the transition point between the Victorian and the modern building style. On the inside, after extensive renovations, it is now a gallery with works dating from the time the house was built. If you're not particularly interested in art go straight outside, as there are fabulous views of Lake Windermere! *Daily 10.30am–5pm | admission £8 | B5360, Bowness-on-Windermere | www.blackwell.org.uk*

BROCKHOLE (126 B2) (📖 E6)

The official visitor centre of the Lake District National Park (4 km/2.5 mi northwest of Bowness) has become a genuine attraction. It has mini golf, treetop challenges, a large garden, and you can hire bicycles and boats here too. In summer a special ferry for bikes, the Bark Barn Bike Boat, runs between Brockhole and the western shore of Lake Windermere. *Admission free | The Lake District Visitor Centre | Brockhole | tel. 015394 4 66 01 | www.lakedistrict.gov.uk*

LAKESIDE (126 B3) (📖 E8)

When you've had enough of boats, you can change to an old steam train at the southern end of Lake Windermere. The ⭐ *Lakeside and Haverthwaite Railway (April–Oct 11.15am–4.50pm approx. hourly | £4.20 per route | www.lakesiderailway.co.uk)* runs old steam engines from the jetty along a 5.6 km/3.5 mi route from Newby Bridge to Haverthwaite. There are inexpensive combined tickets for the train and boat to Ambleside! Right next door at the *Aquarium of the Lakes (daily 10am–4.30pm | admission £6.95 | www.lakesaquarium.co.uk)* fish from the region, including trout and pike, live together in several vast tanks. The *Stott Park Bobbin Mill (April–June, Sept/Oct. Wed–Sun, July/ Aug daily 10am–5pm | admission £7.60 | Finsthwaite | www.english-heritage.org.uk)* is the only remaining working bobbin mill left in the Lake District today, and is open to visitors.

NEWBY BRIDGE (126 B3–4) (📖 E8)

The small village at the southern end of Lake Windermere got its name from the five-arched stone bridge across the River Leven. There isn't a lot to see, but a pint enjoyed outside the elegant *The Swan Hotel (52 rooms | tel. 015395 3 16 81 | www.swanhotel.com | Expensive)* right next to the bridge is one of the most relaxing things you will do in the entire Lake District. Also close by is the INSIDER TIP *Millerbeck Light Railway (Millerbeck House | Staveley-in-Cartmel | www.millerbeck.org.uk)*, a private narrow-gauge railway that runs on special occasions and Bank Holidays. Not far, on the A590, is the ⬤ *Lakeland Motor Museum (daily in summer from 9.30am–5.30pm, otherwise until 4.30pm | admission £8.50| Old Blue Mill | www.lakelandmotormuseum.co.uk)*: a dream for all car lovers. It has hundreds of classic cars, motorbikes and other exhibits, including old Bentleys, Jaguars and even a Trabant.

CARTMEL

(126 B4) (M E8) Welcome to the most hedonistic village in England – in the nicest possible way, of course. Cartmel (pop. 500) lies just outside the Lake District, along its southernmost edge – so is often overlooked.

The entire town is not just idyllic but above all is a paradise for gourmets. Beer is brewed here, and cheese made. There are no fewer than five pubs and their menus can easily hold their own against the smartest restaurants. Best of all: one of the top restaurants in England, *L'Enclume* is situated here. It also has the highest density of smart cars, which are lining the streets.

Full steam ahead through the countryside: Lakeside and Haverthwaite Railway

SIGHTSEEING

CARTMEL PRIORY

For almost 800 years, the church at Cartmel was in the middle of the village – and it soared above everything else for miles around. The medieval priory is well-known for one feature in particular: the extension to the tower sits at a 45-degree angle to the base on which it rests. No one knows exactly why, but it is believed to be unique in England. Be sure to visit – on rainy days in particular, it is a haven of relaxation. The large east window with partly coloured glass dates back to the 15th century and allows plenty of light in, which is also an unusual feature. *In winter daily 9am–3.30pm, otherwise Mon–Sat 9am–5.30pm, Sun until 4.30pm | admission free | Priest Lane | www.cartmelpriory.org.uk*

CARTMEL RACECOURSE ★

England's smallest racecourse is also one of the loveliest. Located on the outskirts of the town, it adds a certain touch of city flair to the area on race days. The traffic is congested for miles as thousands of people head here from every corner of the country. The racecourse itself is only in action on a few days between May and August, usually around Bank Holidays. The races are only part of the experience; many people mainly come for the big party that takes place around the beer and food stands. Do not park in the main car park, but ● INSIDER TIP go to the one at the back – it's free. And if you only want to watch and not bet, then you can also do that here – with the best view, and free of charge. *Admission on race days £15 or £24, depending on the category (cheaper online), otherwise free | www.cartmel-racecourse.co.uk*

CARTMEL

Big show on England's smallest race course – Cartmel Racecourse

FOOD & DRINK

L'ENCLUME ☺
Hidden away, but well worth the search. Simon Rogan's elegant restaurant has already won numerous awards, including two Michelin stars. Sophisticated British cuisine, made with local products. Every single plate is a work of art, but of course it comes at a price. There are also a number of INSIDER TIP very smart rooms for overnight stays. *Cavendish Street | tel. 015395 3 63 62 | www.lenclume.co.uk | Expensive*

THE KINGS ARMS ☺
This lovely old pub in a central location has perfected British pub food – even a basic pleasure such as a prawn sandwich is presented artistically. Regional products, many organic. *The Square | tel.* 015395 3 32 46 | kingsarmshawkshead. co.uk | Expensive

SHOPPING

Something for the sweet-toothed: even superstar Madonna is said to have sampled the sticky toffee pudding from Cartmel. This is a popular export for the village and is available from the *Village Shop (The Square)* where it is also made. Home-brewed beer is available from INSIDER TIP *Unsworth's Yard Brewery (4 Unsworth's Yard)* and opposite at *Hotwines (5a Unsworth's Yard)*.

LEISURE & SPORTS

Starting at the racecourse and moving west for 6 km/3.7 mi is a ⤵ circular route which offers good views of the town, and passes fields and tiny *Mount Barnard*. If you want something longer: the 39 km/24.2 mi *Cistercian Way* takes you from Grange-over-Sands through Cartmel to the coast at Barrow-in-Furness.

Or would you rather take to the air? A parachute jump promises to be more of a buzz: *Sky Dive Northwest (tandem jump £230 | Cark Airfield | Moor Lane | Flookburgh | tel. 015395 5 86 72 | www. skydivenorthwest.co.uk)* operates to the north of Cartmel.

WHERE TO STAY

PRIORY HOTEL
The rooms in this old but very comfortable hotel have been carefully updated. It is in the middle of Cartmel. *7 rooms | The Square | tel. 015395 3 40 70 | www. prioryhotelcartmel.co.uk | Expensive*

WHERE TO GO

GRANGE-OVER-SANDS
(126 B4–5) (*⌐ E8*)
This pretty seaside resort (pop. 4000) has developed on the southern edge of the Lake District, where the River Kent flows into Morecambe Bay. In the 19th century, the railway connection turned the fishing village into something of a spa resort. The salty sea air was believed to be beneficial, especially for tuberculosis sufferers. Although sometimes you have to search for the sea: the tides are the reason for the suffix "over Sands" – more photographs are taken of the sand banks when the tide is out than when it is in.

There is one thing you will find in abundance in this chic holiday resort: peace. The traffic-free promenade is ideal for a walk. The Victorian *Cumbria Grand Hotel (124 rooms | Lindale Road | tel. 015395*

3 23 31 | *www.strathmorehotels.com* | *Expensive)* is the best hotel in town. Good British cuisine ranging from beef to vegetarian gratins is served at the *Thyme Out Restaurant (Main Street | tel. 015395 3 40 79 | www.thymeoutgrange. com | Moderate)*.

HOLKER ESTATE (126 B4–5) (*⌐ E8*)
This country house in the Jacobean Revival style situated 4 km/2.5 mi to the south-west is privately owned by the Cavendish family, one of the most influential aristocratic families in England, and also the owner of the racecourse in Cartmel. Although the turrets and towers on the outside are well worth a visit, the magnificent rooms inside are almost without equal. Silk-covered ceilings, extensive wood carvings and 3500-year-old books in the library are other good reasons for a visit. The formal gardens comprise 10 hectares, and are well known for their large rhododendrons and old trees. Every year in late spring, the Holker Estate holds a spring fair with lots of attractions. *April–Oct Wed–Sun 10.30am–5pm | admission £12.50 | Cark-in-Cartmel | www.holker.co.uk*

GRASMERE

MAP INSIDE BACK COVER
(126 B1) (*⌐ E6*) **The ultimate in picture perfect: in Grasmere (pop. 1000) the few streets wind their way around the village and cows are frequently seen strolling through the centre.**

If you need an ATM, keep an eye on the opening times of the only – and very small – supermarket. That's the only place where you can get cash out. People come here by the coachload for short stays, on pilgrimages to learn more about the life and times of the poet William Wordsworth, who lived in the area for quite some time. Everyone else is pleased to be in a film worthy village with endless opportunities for walking in the surrounding area. If possible, stay overnight – come the evening, the day visitors will have gone, and then it becomes truly idyllic.

SIGHTSEEING

ALLAN BANK ★ ☼ (U D4) (*Ⅲ d4*)

An unusual historic building: help yourself to tea or coffee from the kitchen, and make yourself at home in what used to be the home of Canon Rawnsley. The co-founder of the National Trust once lived here, and poet William Wordsworth is said to have found inspiration within these walls. The lack of wallpaper and fancy furniture gives the building a very special atmosphere. Many of the rooms have wonderful views of Lake Grasmere, and you can sit wherever you like, including the ● deck chairs in the garden. A film in a separate building tells the history of the house in a highly informative way. Go out the back door and stroll for about 1 km/ 0.6 mi around the grounds, through a Victorian tunnel and up a steep hill. *March–Oct daily 10am–5pm, Nov/Dec Fri–Tue 10am–4pm | admission £6, £10 | Broad Gate | www.nationaltrust. org.uk*

DOVE COTTAGE ★ (U F6) (*Ⅲ f6*)

The poet William Wordsworth started his family in this former inn on the edge of Grasmere. Visiting today, you can see how modestly the family lived in those days. Join one of the tours and even experts on Wordsworth are sure to learn a number of interesting facts about the poet's life, and life in days gone by. Next door, the *Wordsworth Museum (admission included)* contains pictures and manuscripts of the writer's past. *March–Oct daily 9.30am–5.30pm, Nov–Feb 10am–4.30pm | admission £8.95 | www.wordsworth.org.uk*

FOOD & DRINK

INSIDER TIP ▶ BALDRY'S TEA ROOM ● ◐ (U E5) (*Ⅲ e5*)

This little café makes you feel like you are in your grandmother's living room. It serves cakes, sandwiches, soup and cream tea with scones and clotted cream, and almost everything is made using local products. In good weather, you can sit outside and enjoy watching life in Grasmere. *Red Lion Square | tel. 07760 773671 | www. baldryscottage.co.uk | Budget*

FOREST SIDE ◐ (U E5) (*Ⅲ e5*)

Kevin Tickle is a Cumbrian and a chef – both by conviction. For decades, he has been producing carefully balanced Anglo-French meals made from local products. He often uses herbs and vegetables from his own garden. *Keswick Road | tel. 015394 35250 | www.the forestside.com | Expensive*

SHOPPING

All visitors head to *Sarah Nelson's Gingerbread Shop* (U E5) (*Ⅲ e5*) (*Church Cottage | www.grasmeregingerbread.co.uk*) – all you have to do is look out for the queue outside a tiny cottage next to the cemetery. Although the original Sarah Nelson is long gone, the gingerbread is still mixed and freshly baked here every day: a unique, spicy-sweet cross between a biscuit and a cake. Of course, the recipe is a closely-guarded secret!

Pack a picnic and get your boots on: walking at Grasmere

LEISURE & SPORTS

Rowing boats are available to hire from *Faeryland* (U D6) *(ጠ d6)* *(£15 per hour | Red Bank Road | tel. 015394 35060 | www.faeryland.co.uk)* on the outskirts of the town.

Lake Grasmere's size makes it ideal for about an hour's walk, even though there isn't a path close to the lake at the northwest, and you have to take a detour along a narrow side street for a short distance.

About an hour's walk – access via Easedale Road next to the *Heaton Cooper Studio* (U D4) *(ጠ d4)* – will take you to beautiful ★●⌇ *Easedale Tarn*. Even on the way up, the views of the valley are breathtaking. A wonderful stillness awaits you at the top – thanks in part to the fact that there is no mobile phone reception up here at all. The main thing is: you have found the perfect spot for your picnic!

WHERE TO STAY

THE INN (U D5) *(ጠ d5)*
This charmingly updated, traditional hotel with one of the village's few pubs, is located right at the centre. From the ⌇ balconies in the rooms upstairs you have INSIDERTIP a lovely view of Grasmere. *49 rooms | Red Lion Square | tel. 0844 3876068 | www.grasmere redlionhotel.co.uk | Moderate*

Lake Elterwater is even more stunning in winter

THE WORDSWORTH HOTEL
(U D5) (🗺 d5)

Although the name is all this hotel shares with the famous poet William Wordsworth, the location in the middle of the village is just as impressive as his works. Lovely rooms, excellent food. *39 rooms | Church Stile | tel. 015394 3 55 92 | www.thewordsworthhotel.co.uk | Expensive*

INFORMATION

Tourist Information (U D5) (🗺 d5) *| Red Bank Road | tel. 015394 3 52 45*

WHERE TO GO

ELTERWATER AND GREAT LANGDALE
(126 A–B 1–2) (🗺 D–E6)

A concealed village not far from the eponymous lake that is often used as the setting for British countryside murder mysteries. Elterwater in the Great Langdale valley is only accessible via narrow roads – but it's worth the effort. There is a good track down to the lake, and in the village itself (pop. 100). Weather permitting you can sit outside *Elterwater Café* and enjoy a cappuccino. For a pint head across the road to the *Britannia Inn (tel. 015394 3 72 10 |*

Budget), which also serves typical pub food. You can park a little further down the road, in the National Trust car park (often full). At the side, there is access to Elterwater down an approximately 700 m/230 ft long path along the River Brathay. All of Langdale is perfect for walking. There are several holiday apartments, with one particularly comfortable one being *Jonty's Cottage (1 room | 1 Main Street | tel. 015394 37417 | www.jontyscottage. co.uk | Moderate)*.

RYDAL MOUNT (126 B1) (*ω E6*)

You can't help but get creative in this village 3 km/1.9 mi south of Grasmere. The last home of the poet William Wordsworth is the perfect retreat. Situated high above Rydal Water, it used to offer fabulous views of the lake. Today, though, and especially in summer, the views are blocked by the trees but that doesn't make it any less attractive. It is now owned by the writer's great-granddaughter and is open to visitors. You can follow Wordsworth's footsteps through the fully-furnished rooms, admire the beautifully preserved furniture, and above all enjoy the flower garden. INSIDER TIP *Rydal Hall (30 rooms | Rydal | tel. 015394 32050 | Moderate)* opposite is a Christian conference centre, belonging to the Diocese of Carlisle, on a wonderful estate that dates back to the 16th century. Overnight accommodation is available to all. *Rydal Mount: March–Oct daily 9.30am– 5pm, Nov–Feb Wed–Sun 11am–4pm | admission £7.50 | www.rydalmount.co.uk*

KENDAL

 MAP INSIDE BACK COVER (126–127 C–D3) (*ω F–G7*) The little town of Kendal (pop. 29,000) is the southern centre of the Lake District, although it lies a little outside the National Park.

If you like convenience, this is the place for you – a pretty little pedestrian zone, lots of restaurants, a cinema and shopping centres – and you can explore the Lake District on day trips. Kendal itself also has a couple of sights, including an old castle ruin. And the town has another benefit: accommodation, meals and petrol are INSIDER TIP often cheaper here than in the National Park itself.

SIGHTSEEING

KENDAL CASTLE ⚶ (U C2) (*ω c2*)

Don't wear your best shoes to explore the ruins of Kendal castle – the path up to it is almost always muddy, but it's definitely worth the effort. The 12th century walls are perfect for photos, and that's not all: from up here, you have wonderful views of Kendal and the surrounding mountains. Only a few walls remain of the actual castle. *Always open | admission free | Castle Hill | Access via Sunnyside*

MUSEUM OF LAKELAND LIFE AND INDUSTRY (U B3) (*ω b3*)

Perfect for a rainy day: this well-organised museum of local history explains the history of the Lake District. Utensils and pictures illustrate how people lived by mining, farming and the textile industry long before the tourists started coming here. *Mon–Sat 10.30am–5pm | admission £5.50 | Abbot Hall Art Gallery | Kirkland | www.lakelandmuseum.org.uk*

FOOD & DRINK

CASTLE DAIRY ● (U B1) (*ω b1*)

Fine, multiple-award winning food is served in this medieval listed building: from lamb and rabbit to fish, everything is perfectly prepared and presented. *26 Wildman Street | tel. 01539 814756 | www.castledairy.co.uk | Moderate*

DÉJÀ-VU IN KENDAL (U A1) (*☉ a1*)
This tiny bistro on the outskirts of the shopping street is famous for its reasonably-priced menu offering fish, meat and vegetarian dishes. *124 Stricklandgate | tel. 01539 72 48 43 | www.dejavukendal. com | Moderate*

SHOPPING
The centre of Kendal leaves almost nothing to be desired. The old market (U A1) (*☉ a1*) has been converted into a shopping centre. There are still some market stalls but nowadays they only sell knickknacks. There are food stands just outside the main door on Wednesday and Saturday mornings.

LEISURE & SPORTS
Although Kendal is not in the mountains, it does have the *Lakeland Climbing Centre* (0) (*☉ 0*) *(admission £10.50 | Lake District Business Park | Mint Bridge Road | tel. 01539 72 17 66 | www.kend alwall.co.uk)* with an artificial climbing wall.
There are cycle routes from Kendal to Lake Windermere and Bowness (16 km/ 9.9 mi), as well as to Arnside on the coast (42 km/26.1 mi) – although due to the lack of cycle paths they are almost always on roads. There is no cycle hire in Kendal, so you either need to bring your own or hire in Windermere.

WHERE TO STAY
MILLERS BECK COUNTRY GUESTHOUSE (0) (*☉ 0*)
Basic B&B outside Kendal, self-catering also possible. *4 rooms | Millers Beck*

Millbridge Lane | Stainton | Kendal | tel. 01539 56 08 77 | www.millersbeck.co.uk | Budget

THE RIVERSIDE (U B1) (*☉ b1*)
A comfortable hotel with a spa, situated in a converted 17th century tannery next to the river. *50 rooms | Stramongate Bridge | Beezon Road | tel. 01539 73 48 61 | www.riversidekendal.co.uk | Moderate*

INFORMATION
Kendal Tourist Information Centre Made in Cumbria (U B2) (*☉ b2*) *| 48A Branthwaite Brow | tel. 01539 73 58 91 | www.visitcum bria.com/sl/kendal*

WHERE TO GO
HAWKSHEAD BREWERY (126 C2) (*☉ F7*)
Although the copper brewing tank instantly catches the eye, it's the contents that really count: on a tour of the Hawkshead Brewery (8 km/5 mi north-west of Kendal) you'll learn what makes Cumbrian beer so hoppy, and why some varieties even contain fruit and spices. And then comes the tasting – for instance, a fruity Windermere Pale Ale, a fresh, light Hawkshead lager or even a malty Red. Whichever you choose, they all have far more flavour than the usual supermarket beers. There is also a *restaurant (Moderate)* that is open every day and serves all the beers that are brewed here. *Tours daily 1pm | admission £8 | Staveley Mill Yard | Unit 22/28, Back Lane | Staveley | tel. 01539 82 26 44 | www.hawkshead brewery.co.uk*

LEVENS HALL (126 C4) (*☉ F8*)
The gardens of this Elizabethan estate make for a special experience: the

Benches in a sea of flowers: the centuries-old garden of Levens Hall

focal point is the unique collection of ancient and extraordinary topiary characters. Guillaume Beaumont, one-time gardener to James II, designed the garden at the end of the 17th century, and large sections of it have been maintained to this day.

Much of the building is even older, and in fact dates back to the 13th century. Inside, the lavishly furnished rooms are of particular interest, as are the artistically decorated ceilings throughout and the leather-covered walls of the dining room. There's even more nature on the other side of the road – the large park is full of deer. *April–Sept Sun–Thu noon–4pm (gardens 10am–5pm) | admission £13.50 | www.levenshall.co.uk*

SIZERGH CASTLE ● (126 C3) (*Ⅲ F7*)

This beautifully-preserved, 750-year-old castle stands a short distance from Kendal – sadly the inside can only be seen on guided tours given at strictly controlled times. Yet the detailed wood panelling and large entrance hall are well worth a visit. A tour will take you past old portraits and rare furniture. There is also a 16th century bedchamber, the Inlaid Chamber, that was sold to the Victoria and Albert Museum in the 1890s and displayed as a reconstructed period room before finally being returned to its original home in 1999. The gardens are open all year round, and contain hundreds of plants from the surrounding area. There is also an orchard and hardy ferns which are part of the National Collection. Nearby you can find the ☻ INSIDER TIP *Farm Shop (Low Sizergh Barn)* – be sure to call in! As well as gifts and local produce, you can also enjoy a delicious snack in the café. *Sizergh Castle Gardens daily from 10am–5pm | guided tours of the house April–Oct Tue–Fri, Sun 11am and 11.20am (£1) | admission £10.50 | www.nationaltrust.org.uk*

CONISTON WATER & THE SOUTH WEST

In the mood for something different? Some of the most beautiful mountains create a breathtaking landscape in the south west of the Lake District.

Most of Cumbria's main industries are to be found along the coast. The main one is the rather unattractive Sellafield power station providing jobs for over 10,000 people, while Barrow-in-Furness is one of the leading shipyards in England. However, the contrast is hardly noticeable, because visitors rarely go to the industrial areas; everything worth seeing is a long way away.

There are several lakes in the south west, namely Coniston Water, Wast Water and Tarn Hows that are ideal for short walks. The views of the surrounding mountains from Hardknott Pass are impressive, and time and again you'll come across the historical heritage of Romans and Celts. The south west may be quieter than other regions, but that's not to say it's any less exciting.

CONISTON

(125 E2) (∅ D7) **The mines around this old mining town (pop. 900) closed many years ago, but the grey slate-tiled houses still bear witness to those days.** Coniston to the north west of the lovely Coniston Water is well established as a tourist destination. A number of cafés, pubs and souvenir shops line the main B5286. They are perfect for sitting outside in the summer. But don't get too settled – it's even nicer next to the water.

An idyll amongst mountains and coast – the south west of the Lake District is varied and not overrun

RUSKIN MUSEUM

A somewhat different local museum: as the name implies, the Ruskin Museum tells the story of the life of the writer John Ruskin, who was born in this area. However, it's not just about literature, but also about curiosities and speciali-ties of the region such as copper mines, violins and the *Bluebird K7*. This particu-lar "blue bird" is Donald Campbell's trail-blazing jet-engined hydroplane. He was killed in an accident in it on Coniston Wa-ter in 1967. The museum contains pho-tos and texts as well as a lot of excellent exhibits. *Mid March–mid Nov daily from 10am–4.30pm | admission £6 | A593 | www.ruskinmuseum.com*

STEAM YACHT GONDOLA ★ ●

In the warmer summer months, you can enjoy a pleasant ride across Coniston Water in this steam-powered yacht – exactly as passengers on the Furness Railway would have experienced in the

19th century. The Furness Railway originally had the *Steam Yacht* built as an extension to the railway line.

You can still experience a great deal of the flair of those days when you are on-board. *April–Oct daily, usually four*

Seeing which way the wind blows on the Steam Yacht Gondola

sailings (11am, noon, 1pm and 2.30pm) | Ticket prices from £11 | Coniston Pier | Lake Road | www.nationaltrust.org.uk

FOOD & DRINK

THE BLACK BULL INN

The food that is served in this pub is good, filling stuff: lamb, fish & chips and satisfying desserts such as brownies. Fortunately, it can all be washed down with a genuine **INSIDER TIP** *Coniston Ale* which is brewed in several versions on the premises of this pub. *The Lake District | tel. 015394 4 13 35 | www.blackbullconiston.co.uk | Moderate*

BLUEBIRD CAFÉ

Make yourself comfortable and gaze at the water – or at the boats that are constantly mooring up and casting off from here. The café is in the perfect location right on the banks of Coniston Water, and has an excellent menu that includes cakes, pasta, salads and sandwiches. *Lake Road | tel. 015394 4 16 49 | www.thebluebirdcafe.co.uk | Budget*

LEISURE & SPORTS

Rowing, paddling, cycling – Coniston Water is ideal for all sorts of activities. Boats and bikes are available to hire on the lake from *Coniston Boating Centre (daily from 10am–5pm | from £15/hour/boat or two hours/bike | Lake Road | tel. 015394 4 13 66 | www.conistonboatingcentre.co.uk)*.

A popular and not too challenging walk takes you from Coniston to the ☼ *Old Man,* a peak with spectacular views, in about two hours.

WHERE TO STAY

BANK GROUND FARM

An enchanting old but modernised farmhouse on the eastern side of Coniston Water with comfortable B&B rooms and six holiday apartments. *6 rooms | Coniston Water | tel. 015394 4 12 64 | www.bankground.com | Budget*

WATERHEAD HOTEL

From the ☼ terrace you have views of the mountains and – slightly hidden by trees – Coniston Water: Peace and relaxation are the order of the day in this lovely, old English hotel. *24 rooms |*

Hawkshead Road | tel. 01539 44 12 44 | www.waterhead-hotel.co.uk | Moderate

INFORMATION

Tourist Information Centre | Ruskin Ave | tel. 015394 4 15 33 | www.conistontic.org

WHERE TO GO

BRANTWOOD ⬇ (125 E2–3) *(ጠ E7)*

Once the home of the writer and philosopher John Ruskin, this is now a museum and arts centre. It is beautifully located on the eastern side of Coniston Water, with views of the lake and the mountains behind. You'll be hard pushed to find anywhere nicer to stay. The inside still looks exactly as it did in Ruskin's day. He lived here in the Lake District from 1871 until his death in 1900. It's best to travel on the INSIDER TIP Coniston Launch boats *(daily and hourly from 11am–3pm | Trips from £11.25 | www.conistonlaunch. co.uk)* from Coniston Pier across the lake to Brantwood; the trip across the water is an experience in itself. The beautifully refurbished *Terrace Coffee House (Budget)* serves lovely snacks all day long, and guests can also sit outside and enjoy the view of the mountains. *March–Nov daily 10.30am–5pm, Dec–Feb 10.30am–4pm | admission £7.70 (garden only £5.35) | discount if arriving by boat, voucher with ticket purchase | Coniston Water east side | www.brantwood.org.uk*

GRIZEDALE FOREST
(125 E–F 2–3) *(ጠ E7)*

This famous woodland between Coniston Water and Windermere is not only known as a recreation area, but above all for its *sculpture trail (www.grize dalesculpture.org)*, with a permanent display of around 40 pieces by international artists scattered throughout the forest. You can see most of them along the *Silurian Way,* a 16 km/ 9.9 mi circular trail around Grizedale. The visitor centre between Hawkshead and Penny Bridge is a good starting point. You can also hire mountain and electric bikes here *(£25–40 per day | tel. 01229 86 03 35 | www.velobikes. co.uk)* – the best option for a sporty experience of Grizedale. *www.forestry.gov. uk/grizedale*

TARN HOWS ⬇ (125 E2) *(ጠ E6)*

Although Tarn Hows (actually *The Tarns*) is only a relatively small lake, its many islands and wooded surroundings make it one of the most photographed lakes in the entire Lake District. It's best to

---

MARCO POLO HIGHLIGHTS

⭐ **Hoad Monument**
Looks light a lighthouse but it isn't – there are fabulous views from this monument high above Ulverston → p. 57

⭐ **Muncaster Castle**
Country house with a touch of haunted castle about it – and a large garden → p. 56

⭐ **Ravenglass and Eskdale Railway**
This old railway line runs from Ravenglass through wonderful countryside → p. 54

⭐ **Hardknott Pass**
A steep mountain pass with fabulous views of the mountains → p. 56

⭐ **Steam Yacht Gondola**
Sail across Coniston Water on this old steam ship → p. 51

walk there to make the most of the charming narrow roads and surrounding nature – situated about 4 km/ 2.5 mi from Coniston or Hawkshead. There is a circular walk around the lake. Like so many parts of the Lake District, Tarn Hows once belonged to the writer Beatrix Potter. However, she sold the lake to the National Trust while she was still alive.

RAVENGLASS

(124 C2) (*m C7*) **Welcome to the only coastal village and natural harbour** **(pop. 1200) in the National Park – all the others are just outside the park.**

Here, at the estuary of three rivers, the Esk, Mite and Irt just before the sea, is a completely different part of the Lake District. The smell of the sea and seaweed is in the air, and a few boats lie at anchor as seagulls circle overhead. Daily life in Ravenglass is so tranquil that you probably won't want to leave – after all, you wouldn't want to disturb anyone.

In former days, iron ore mined from the hills above Boot was transferred from a siding to the main line. Today the village still profits from the railway, albeit now as a tourist attraction. It's a short walk from the station to the ruins of an ancient Roman Bath House *(Walls Drive)*, of which sadly only little remains.

LOW BUDGET

If you are planning on spending some time around Coniston Water and setting off from various starting points, it might make sense to purchase a *weekly ticket for the Coniston Launch boats (available on the jetty and online | www.conistonlaunch. co.uk)*: for £26, you can spend a week travelling the length and breadth of it, whereas a single day will set you back between £11 and £12.50, depending on the route.

Save on your food and support local farmers at the same time: at the *farmers markets*, farmers bring their products straight to the customer – often at surprisingly reasonable prices, and cheaper than the supermarkets. Almost all of the bigger towns have one, and there's a lovely one on the third Saturday of the month in the middle of Ulverston *(9.30am–2.30pm | Market Street)*.

FOOD & DRINK

THE INN AT RAVENGLASS

You really must get a 🌿 window seat in this pub – the view of the estuary will instantly have you dreaming. But please don't forget about the excellent food that is served here, from scallops to lamb. Also has a number of rooms *(Moderate)*. *Main Street | tel. 01229 71 72 30 | theinnatravenglass.co.uk | Moderate*

LEISURE & SPORTS

The old steam train of the ★ ● 🌿 *Ravenglass and Eskdale Railway (April– Oct daily up to 13 departures, Feb/March and Dec weekends only, daily in school holidays | Return £13.90 | www.ravenglass-railway.co.uk)* travels east for 11.3 km/ 7 mi through the beautiful countryside along the tracks of an old industrial train to Dalegarth for Boot. You'll see the peaks of the Lake District, lots of idyllic farmland and – above all – sheep. The

Past the peaks and farmland on the Ravenglass and Eskdale Railway

train is named after an old Cumbrian word, *La'al Ratty,* little railway, or simply "Ratty". If you also want to see Muncaster Castle, you can buy a combined ticket for £24! From Dalegarth there are walking trails for every ability, with the most challenging one heading up the 393 m/ 1,289 ft ☆ Hardknott Pass. After heading east for about 1.5 km/0.9 mi you'll come to the INSIDER TIP ▶ *Hardknott Café (Hardknott Pass | Eskdale | tel. 019467 2 32 30 | www.woolpack.co.uk | Moderate)* with good pub food, lots of beers and excellent coffee, while the *Woolpack Inn (Budget)* next door also has several basic but modern rooms.

There is a circular walk of around 6 km/3.7 mi from Dalegarth station through Eskdale to *Doctor's Bridge* and back again in a curve via Stanley Force to Dalegarth.

WHERE TO STAY

PENNINGTON HOTEL
No frills but a guesthouse with bright, modern rooms – ☆ some even with views of the estuary. Serves good pub food. *19 rooms | Main Street | www.penningtonhotel.co.uk | Moderate*

INFORMATION

Tourist Information | Train Station | tel. 01229 71 72 78

WHERE TO GO

BLACK COMBE (124 C4) *(♍ C8)*
According to the locals, this mountain is so easy to climb, you could even do so in your slippers. The 600 m colossus is on Cumbria's south west coast. In fact, it

really is easy (two to three hours there and back), and no special equipment is required. The best starting point for the Black Combe is the little coastal resort of *Silecroft*, which you can also reach by train. There isn't much to see there apart from a small, very basic pub, the *Miners Arms (Main Street | tel. 012 29 77 23 25 | www.minersarmssilecroft. com | Moderate)*. The extensive menu (traditional British fare) includes a surprising number of vegetarian dishes.

HARDKNOTT PASS ★ ☼
(125 D2) (*ω D6*)

Those who choose to drive Hardknott Pass should have some experience of driving in mountains: the relatively narrow road – mostly single-track – is the steepest road in England with a maximum gradient of 1 in 3. But it's worth

it: you'll be greeted by one of the most impressive mountain views in the entire Lake District! The mountain pass winds up like a river, in tight hairpin bends, to an altitude of 393 m/1,289 ft. The Romans built the road in the 2nd century. Half way up, at about 200 m/656 ft is a reminder of them in the form of the foundation walls of an old *fort (Hardknott Roman Fort | Always accessible | admission free | Hardknott Pass | Eskdale | www.eng lish-heritage.org.uk)*. Towards Ambleside, the road joins the equally lovely Wrynose Pass, which connects Duddon Valley and Little Langdale.

MUNCASTER CASTLE ★ ☼
(124 C2) (*ω C7*)

Not unlike a haunted castle, Muncaster Castle sits on a hill just outside Ravenglass, surrounded by over 74 acres of

Eye to eye with a peregrine falcon: display at Muncaster Castle

gardens and forest. The castle plays on its haunted image, although you have absolutely nothing to fear: it has been the home of the Pennington family for 800 years, and they have furnished the rooms exquisitely with rare furniture, large works of art and wood panelling. You can visit the castle (in summer only), walk around the gardens, and experience one of several daily bird of prey displays at the owl and falconry centre. There are evening events in the week up to Halloween and around Christmas, and these do include a little bit of spookiness. For a more immersive experience at Muncaster Castle, you can INSIDER TIP sleep on the premises: the former coach houses have been converted into comfortable *B&B rooms (10 rooms | Moderate). Muncaster | Ravenglass | daily from 11am–4pm (5pm in summer), castle only April–Oct Sun–Fri noon–4pm | admission £14 | www.muncaster.co.uk*

WASDALE

(124–125 C–D 1–2) *(🕮 C–D 5–6)*

The lake *Wast Water,* at 79 m the deepest lake in England, covers vast areas of the Wasdale. The valley is surrounded by stunning views, grass covered rocks, heathers and countless streams. Sheep graze amongst the centuries-old dry stone walls. The valley is bordered by *Scafell Pike, Great Gable, Kirk Fell* and *Red Pike,* some of the highest mountains in England.

The National Trust maintains several romantic *cottages here (www.nationaltrust.org.uk | Moderate)* as self-catering properties, as well as a campsite on the north east shore that also has a number of INSIDER TIP pods for overnight stays. The *Wasdale Head Inn (Wasdale Head | Gosforth | tel. 019467 26229 | www.wasdale.com | Budget),* a basic pub at the north east end of the valley, serves good, plain pub food.

ULVERSTON

(125 E4–5) *(🕮 D–E 8–9)* **The people in Ulverston (pop. 12,000) have a very famous son: Stan Laurel, the skinny half of the comedy duo Laurel and Hardy, grew up here.**

There is a statue of the two outside the *Coronation Hall* theatre as well as an entire museum. By Cumbrian standards, Ulverston is almost like a city. Don't be put off by the main road, even though it can get congested at rush hour. The centre consists of a maze of narrow streets and a pretty little pedestrian zone with lots of shops.

SIGHTSEEING

HOAD MONUMENT ★

What looks like a lighthouse high above the town is simply a memorial: Sir John Barrow, British politician, admiral and co-founder of the Royal Geographic Society, was born in Ulverston. Locals built the 30 m/98.4 ft tower, which is also called the Sir John Barrow Monument, in his honour. There are 112 narrow steps to get to the top and – as you would expect – wonderful views of the town and water. The construction never actually was a lighthouse, as it never had the beacon. However, some evenings it is INSIDER TIP lit up in colour to mark special occasions – such as Halloween, New Year's Eve and on 16 June every year, Stan Laurel's birthday, when it is even more photogenic than usual. *April–Oct Sun 1pm–5pm (a raised flag indicates when the tower is open) | admission free | Hoad Hill | Access on foot from Chittery Lane | short.travel/lkd8*

ULVERSTON

LAUREL & HARDY MUSEUM

Stan Laurel and Oliver Hardy really didn't have much to do with England after they went to the USA and started making films there. Despite that, Ulverston pays due consideration – to Stan in particular, who was born here in 1890 and grew up in the town. Collectors have lovingly created a museum in a part of the former Roxy picture house. Old Laurel and Hardy films are shown here on a loop, and the couple's career is explained on information panels. *Nov–March Tue and Thu–Sun, otherwise daily from 10am–5pm | admission £5 | The Roxy | Brogden Street | www.laurel-and-hardy.co.uk*

FOOD & DRINK

THE FARMERS

You're right in the thick of things here: visitors to this rustic pub on the market square are very well fed on burgers, mussels and fisherman's salad. On Thursdays, at the INSIDER TIP weekly quiz night, the entire pub tests its knowledge. Anyone can take part and it's a great chance to get to know the locals. *2 Market Place | tel. 01229 58 44 69 | www.the-farmers-ulverston.co.uk | Moderate*

GILLAM'S

Just like Grandma's: an old coffee house that serves small dishes and delicious cakes, a large selection of teas and its own roasted coffees. There is a separate menu for vegans. *64 Market Street | tel. 01229 58 75 64 | www.gillams-tearoom.co.uk | Budget*

LEISURE & SPORTS

The *Bike Station (bike £20/day | Ulverston Station | tel. 01229 58 78 29 | www.ulverstonbikecafe.co.uk)*, a combination of cycle shop and café, also rents bikes.

WHERE TO STAY

VIRGINIA HOUSE

A small, homely hotel in the centre that also has a terrific gin bar and an excellent restaurant that serves modern European cuisine, with dishes ranging from fish to meat (*Expensive*). *8 rooms | 24 Queen Street | tel. 01229 58 48 44 | www.virginiahouseulverston.co.uk | Moderate*

INFORMATION

Tourist Information | Coronation Hall | County Square | tel. 01229 58 71 20 | www.ulverstoncouncil.org.uk

WHERE TO GO

BARROW-IN-FURNESS
(125 D5–6) (*∅ C–D9*)

The lavish Victorian buildings in the centre tell you that the old harbour town of Barrow-in-Furness (pop. 72,000) once enjoyed great riches. Times have changed: although the buildings are still lovely and much effort was put into updating the pedestrian zone, the shops are struggling. Barrow used to be the biggest iron and steel centre in the world. The town is still an important centre for the ship-building industry today, and in fact has England's only submarine shipyard. The ● *Dock Museum (Wed–Sun 11am–4pm | admission free | North Road | www.dockmuseum.org.uk)* has detailed information on Barrow's maritime development. However, the town is mainly known for the ruins of an old Cistercian abbey: built of red sandstone, *Furness Abbey (April–Sept daily from 10am–6pm | admission £5.40 | Manor Road | www.english-heritage.org.uk)*, built in the 12th century, has been decaying for years, and is threatening to disappear completely in the soft ground.

On shaky ground: the sandstone walls of the abbey at Barrow-in-Furness

However, the gigantic outside walls that still stand bear witness to its impressively long history. As you walk around it, you will hardly notice that the rest of the building is no longer standing. It's a similar situation with *Piel Castle (always accessible | admission free | Piel Island | www. english-heritage.org.uk)*, castle ruins that sit almost majestically on a small island off the coast of Barrow that can only be reached by a ferry in the summer months. INSIDER TIP *The Furness Railway (50 rooms | 76–80 Abbey Road | tel. 01229 824758 | www.jdwetherspoon. com | Moderate)* is an excellent pub in the centre with a large selection of British dishes – and also a hotel: the top floors have a number of modern rooms furnished in the boutique style.

SWINSIDE STONE CIRCLE ⚜
(125 D3) (*∅ C7–8*)

This stone circle is comparatively well-preserved. It is situated on farmland west of Broughton-in-Furness and consists of a total of 55 stones. Only five stones are supposed to have been lost since the Bronze Age; the rest of them have survived.

However, the fact that Swinside is not very well known is due mainly to its hidden location. The stone circle is on private land, but can be clearly seen from the path. You can only get there on foot. *Always accessible | admission free | Swinside Farm leave the A595 at Broadgate; you have to walk the last section (approx. 2 km/1.2 mi), as it is only accessible on foot*

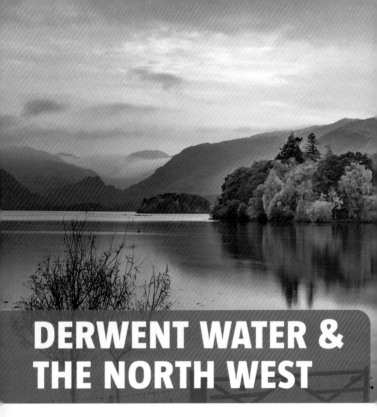

DERWENT WATER & THE NORTH WEST

In the north west of the Lake District, visitors are drawn directly into the valleys or up into the mountains. Some of the peaks still have snow in early spring. The two Buttermeres, for instance, both lake and village, are slightly hidden away in a breathtaking mountain world. Countless sheep graze on the shores of the silent lake, occasionally looking up when someone passes, but otherwise nothing bothers them.

Keswick, one of the most popular towns in the National Park, is somewhere that is constantly on the go. In peak season, coachloads of visitors transform the centre into an oversized ant hill. With lots of little shops, it's the perfect place for shopping.

Cockermouth, not far away to the west, may be quite low down on most people's lists, and yet with its Georgian architecture and numerous little pubs and shops, the birthplace of William Wordsworth is a most underrated destination.

The contrast between the mountains of the Lake District and the Cumbrian Coast could hardly be greater: most visitors tend to forget about the coast – after all, most of them come here to walk and enjoy boat trips. However, harbour towns such as Whitehaven and Maryport have developed into highly confident little towns that are the perfect counterbalance for sheep and mountain views. Centuries ago, goods – mainly rum and spices – arrived here from distant countries. Today, many of the buildings on the coast still exude plenty of this history.

Decisions, decisions – shopping in Keswick or sea views in Whitehaven? The north west has more to offer than just lakes and mountains

BUTTERMERE

(121 D6) *(C
 C5)* **Even by the high standards of the Lake District, this landscape is breathtaking. Buttermere is surrounded by some of the most impressive mountains in the region.**

Drive here via the narrow road between Keswick and Buttermere – the views more than make up for the challenge. When you arrive, you'll find a charming little village: a few farms, old houses,

two pubs and a church. By the time you see children enjoying an ice cream and parents drinking their first pint you'll realise: you are on holiday!

SIGHTSEEING

LAKE BUTTERMERE

Wool warning! Walking along an approximately 1 km/0.6 mi path, you'll pass hundreds of friendly-looking ● Herdwick sheep before you arrive at Lake Buttermere, about 2 km/1.2 mi in length – undeveloped, and unspoilt by tourism. There's an easy walk around the lake which takes about two hours. *Always accessible | admission free | short. travel/lkd9*

ST JAMES' CHURCH

This chapel on a hill on the main street is one of the nicest in the National Park. Even the poet William Wordsworth was full of praise for it. There is a stone me-

but it does offer tender steaks and a couple of vegetarian dishes. And what is even more important for many people: a good selection of real ales. *tel. 017687 70253 | www.fishinnbuttermere.co.uk | Moderate*

SYKE FARM TEA ROOM

Cakes, sandwiches and an excellent English breakfast are available at this farmhouse café. It also makes its own

Original and reflection: mirror-smooth Lake Buttermere

morial to the walker Alfred Wainwright, who was highly regarded in the Lake District. You definitely don't want to miss the east window with biblical motifs, the 19th century organ and the entrance gate, which is made of metal and resembles a garden gate. *Always accessible | admission free*

FOOD & DRINK

THE FISH INN

Despite its name, The Fish Inn – one of the oldest pubs and guesthouses in the Lake District – doesn't serve a lot of fish,

INSIDER TIP delicious ice cream. Sit outside, and you really do feel as if you were in the middle of the countryside. *Syke Farm | B5289 | tel. 017687 70277 | Budget*

LEISURE & SPORTS

Buttermere is a walking area. The most popular tour leads from the town about 13 km/8.1 mi over the mountains *Red Pike, High Stile* and *High Crag* to the *Haystacks* and back. It'll take a day, but it's not at all challenging. If you prefer something easier and shorter, take the ☙ path behind the church up to *Robinson Mountain* (4 km/2.5 mi) – but be warned, it's often damp and muddy. Both options promise fabulous views of the valley!

WHERE TO STAY

BRIDGE HOTEL

Well-established hotel in the middle of Buttermere with beautifully refurbished rooms somewhere between Olde English and ultra-modern style. There is absolute peace and silence come the evening. *21 rooms | B5289 | tel. 017687 7 02 52 | www.bridge-hotel.com | Moderate*

DALEGARTH GUEST HOUSE

Not too much luxury here, but plenty of relaxation: a B&B apparently in the middle of nowhere – but on the lake, and therefore ideal for walkers and anyone who wants to settle down beside the lake with a good book. You can also camp here. *9 rooms | Hassness Estate | tel. 017687 7 02 33 | Budget*

WHERE TO GO

HONISTER PASS ☙ ★
(121 D6) *(ﾑ D5)*

Honister Pass, a breathtaking mountain pass, starts right at the eastern end of Lake Buttermere and heads east to Borrowdale. It goes up to 356 m/1,168 ft, and the walking trails either side go up even higher.

At the head of the pass is *Honister Slate Mine (tours daily at 10.30am, 12.30pm, 3.30pm | admission £13.50 | www.honister.com)* where slate is still mined today. You can view the site, and there are several tours of the tunnels every day. If you'd like to experience the slate up close – secured to the mountain by cable throughout and (hopefully) with a good head for heights – you can climb the *Via Ferrata,* on this fully-guided ascent. Or try the rope bridge – more rope than bridge – that takes you over an abyss at a height of 600 m/1,969 ft.

Right next to the mine is a ☙ **INSIDER TIP** *Youth hostel (March-Oct*

★ **Castlerigg Stone Circle**
The actual stones are almost of secondary importance in this prehistoric stone circle, thanks to the fabulous surrounding area and mountains → p. 70

★ **Ennerdale Water**
One of the lesser-known lakes in the Lake District: original, rough and perfect for walking and cycling → p. 72

★ **Honister Pass**
Slate is still mined today at the top of this spectacular mountain pass → p. 63

★ **Lakes Distillery**
Housed in a beautifully renovated Victorian model farm close to Bassenthwaite Lake, this distillery now produces a single malt whisky → p. 69

★ **Senhouse Roman Museum**
Almost 2000 years ago, the Romans watched over the coast at this point, now this museum in Maryport contains the legacies of those years → p. 73

★ **Derwent Water**
Walking, sailing, relaxing: there's plenty to do on this lake → p. 68

MARCO POLO HIGHLIGHTS

only | 3 dormitories | Honister Pass | Seatoller | tel. 0345 3 71 95 22 (*) | www.yha.org.uk/hostel/yha-honister-hause | *Budget)*, one of the most impressive in England. Not just for its basic interior, but above all for the wonderful views of the Lake District: at the entrance, cast your gaze over the expanse of Borrowdale, sheep grazing alongside, while the only sounds come from the road or, at best, a few tourists – now that's pure relaxation.

LOWESWATER (120 C5–6) *(ⓜ C4–5)*
If you'd like to explore two lakes at the same time, then this little village on the link road between Crummock Water and Loweswater is the best place to start. You'll always have the summit of *Mellbreak* in your sight, but the main destination is ◑ *Kirkstile Inn*

(tel. 01900 8 52 19 | www.kirkstile.com | *Budget)* just off the main road. Not only does it have plenty of beers, but also the best pub food, all made mainly from regional products.

Even inexperienced walkers will find it easy to walk around Loweswater. It is the only lake in the Lake District whose water does not flow directly into the sea via rivers, but remains in the National Park – in neighbouring Crummock Water. The National Trust owns a delightful cottage at the southern end of Loweswater, right next to the lake, INSIDER TIP *Watergate Farm* (3 rooms | Loweswater | tel. 0344 8 00 20 70 (*) | www.nationaltrust.org.uk/holidays | *Moderate)*. At the south west end of the larger lake, Crummock Water, it's well worth taking a walk to *Scale Force*, the highest waterfall in the Lake District.

COCKER-MOUTH

(120 C4–5) *(ⓜ C4)* **At the point where the Cocker flows into the Derwent River, the entirely underestimated small town of Cockermouth (pop. 8000) has developed over the last few centuries.** Often overshadowed by the smaller but far more popular Keswick, it has absolutely no need to hide away. Small, colourful Georgian houses are grouped around the centre. In addition to a large supermarket, you will also find a large number of independent shops. A large market is held on the small *Market Place* once a month *(first Sat in the month, 9am–2pm)*. Partly ruined *Cockermouth Castle* towers over the hill. The castle is still privately owned. It can only be visited on special occasions such as *Cockermouth Festival* or the *Heritage*

A good drop from Cumberland: Jennings Castle Brewery

Open Days (always at the beginning of September).

SIGHTSEEING

JENNINGS CASTLE BREWERY

A jewel in the Lake District crown. This brewery has 190 years of brewing heritage and along with the award winning ales, it forms part of the fabric of the Lake District. On a guide tour you'll learn a lot about the production process and the purity of the Lake District water and will also be able to sample the goods at the end. *Tours (book in advance!) March–Oct Wed–Sat, Nov/Dec, Feb Thu–Sat 1.30pm, shop Mon–Sat 10am–4pm | admission tour £9 | Brewery Lane | tel. 01900 82 03 62 | www.jenningsbrewery.co.uk*

WORDSWORTH HOUSE AND GARDEN

Travel back to 1770 in this Georgian stately home, where the poet William Wordsworth was born. His family lived in this house with their three children and staff, which has now been furnished in the style of the time. Stroll through the furnished rooms, and try your hand at writing with a quill pen as Wordsworth would have done, and finish your visit with a walk through the pretty, clearly laid-out garden. The ☀ INSIDER TIP small café on the top floor serves a good cream tea overlooking Cockermouth's main street. *April–Oct Sat–Thu (also Fri in summer) 11am–5pm | admission £8.40 | 100 Main Street | www.nationaltrust.org.uk*

FOOD & DRINK

HONEST LAWYER

Dine in style: modern British cuisine ranging from fish to steak is served in this former courthouse. Enjoy sitting outside on the narrow balcony next to the river. *2 Main Street | tel. 01900 82 48 88 | www.honestlawyerrestaurant.co.uk | Expensive*

THE SPICE CLUB

Welcome to India: this restaurant on the main road serves excellent curries and delicious naan bread! *25 Main Street |* a hardware store – there is even a small museum in the basement *(Mon–Sat 9am–4pm | admission free)* with lots of memorabilia!

Fancy a change? You'll find shops and cafés in Keswick by Derwent Water

tel. 01900 82 82 88 | www.thespiceclub cockermouth.co.uk | Moderate

SHOPPING

Sainsbury's is the main supermarket but it's not far from here to the *Main Street,* with lots of smaller shops where you're more likely to find practical things rather than the big fashion labels. The *Castlegate House Gallery (Castlegate | www.castlegatehouse.co.uk)* contains an abundance of art from the surrounding area. *JB Banks (13–14 Market Place | www.jbbanks.co.uk)* is much more than

LEISURE & SPORTS

Cyclewise (bicycle from £26/day | Unit 2, Fairfield Buildings | South Street | tel. 01900 82 19 98 | www.cyclewise.co.uk) has all kinds of bikes for hire. Lovely destinations are Buttermere (16 km/9.9 mi) or the coast at Whitehaven (25 km/15.5 mi) – although both routes are hilly.

WHERE TO STAY

ALLERDALE COURT HOTEL

This old, tastefully refurbished hotel is right on the market square. You don't have to be a resident to be welcome in the chic `INSIDER TIP` bar with its excellent afternoon tea. *25 rooms | 18–20 Market Place | tel. 01900 82 36 54 | www.aller dalecourthotel.co.uk | Moderate*

CROFT GUEST HOUSE

A small B&B in the centre with lovingly modernised rooms. And you're part of the family – so you'll pick up the occasional tip on the spot, as it were. Basic but comfortable. *7 rooms | 6–8 Challoner Street | tel. 01900 82 75 33 | www.croft-guesthouse.com | Budget*

Tourist Information Centre | Library | 88 Main Street | tel. 01900 82 26 34 | www.cockermouth.org

WHERE TO GO

ISEL HALL ☆ (120 C4) (*ⓜ C3*)

This spectacular ancient building high above the River Derwent 8 km/5 mi north east of Cockermouth is now a large residence. It is open to the public once a week, and is worth visiting just for the views of the surrounding area. Parts of the estate, including pink *Pele Tower,* date back to the 14th century, although most of it dates back to the 15th and 16th centuries. Of interest inside are old wood panellings, furniture and paintings. *April–Sept Mon 1.30pm–4.30pm, guided tours only | admission £6 | Isel | Bassenthwaite | short.travel/lkd12*

KESWICK

MAP INSIDE BACK COVER
(121 D–E5) (*ⓜ D4*) **You can guess from the sheer number of outdoor**

equipment stores how important **walking and hiking are to this area!**
Keswick (pop. 5000) is the uncontested business centre of the northern Lake District. Countless shops have opened in the centre, not only branches of the major retail groups but also plenty of independent ones. This means that you'll end up here sooner or later, if only when you need to see something other than countryside. However, a visit to Keswick isn't only a good choice for a rainy day. It's also full to bursting in sunshine, and you could have difficulties finding somewhere to sit outside the cafés and restaurants. As Mediterranean as that may seem, Keswick is undeniably Victorian.

SIGHTSEEING

DERWENT PENCIL MUSEUM
(U E1) (*ⓜ e1*)

A museum for pencils? It's not as odd as it sounds. Keswick used to be an important graphite-mining area, which is one of the main constituents of this writing implement. The graphite needed in pencil production was found close by in the 16th century. However, even Keswick wasn't spared structural change, and the factory was closed in 2007. The museum is also home to the biggest colour pencil in the world. It measures almost 8 m/26.2 ft, and was used for marketing purposes. It is now a popular exhibition piece. *Daily from 9.30am–5pm | admission £4.95 | Southey Works | www.pencilmuseum.co.uk*

DERWENT WATER ISLANDS (0) (*ⓜ 0*)

Three small islands in Derwent Water are ideal for escaping the hustle and bustle on land for a day. You can reach them by hiring a boat from one of the boat hire centres on the shore, *St Herbert's* and *Rampsholme Island* are now uninhabited, but they are idyllic spots for reading, thinking and/or a picnic. *Derwent Island* is the only inhabited island, and therefore only accessible to visitors on a number of days a year (current dates at *www.nationaltrust.org.uk/borrowdale-and-derwentwater*).

PUZZLING PLACE (U E2) (🗺 e2)
A world of illusions: this combination of shop and museum plays with optical illusions. Holograms lead you astray, while in the *Anti-Gravity Room* you'll seem to stand at an impossible slant and lean effortlessly into space without falling. Of course, the name says it all: there are puzzles galore! *In winter Tue–Sun (Jan Sat/Sun only), otherwise daily from 11am–5pm | admission £3.75 | 9 Museum Square | www.puzzlingplace.co.uk*

FOOD & DRINK

JAVA COFFEE SHOP (U E2) (🗺 e2)
If you like people-watching, this is the place to come. This small, unassuming café in the pedestrian zone serves delicious coffees, various cakes and a range of snacks – and you can also sit outside for an excellent view of the comings and goings. *23 Main Street | tel. 017687 725 68 | Budget*

MORRELS (U E2) (🗺 e2)
Every plate is a work of art: delicious fish and meat dishes and desserts are beautifully presented at this restaurant. *34 Lake Road | tel. 017687 726 66 | www.morrels.co.uk | Expensive*

SHOPPING

● Most of the shops are on Main Street in the middle of the town. You'll also find local products such as the fragrant soaps of the INSIDER TIP *Soap Company* (U E2) (🗺 e2) (*Main Street | www.the* *soapco-keswick.org*) and food and jams from von *Love the Lakes (6–8 St John's Street | www.lovethelakes.net*).

LEISURE & SPORTS

★ *Derwent Water* is close to the centre of Keswick, and is one of the best-developed lakes in the Lake District. There is a lovely walk around it (13 km/8.1 mi), and *excursion boats* (U E3) (🗺 e3) (*Keswick Launch | March–Oct daily from 10am–4pm (July/Aug also 5pm), Nov–Feb Sat/Sun 11.30am and 2.30pm | Return/ 50 min. £10.50 | tel. 017687 722 63 | www.keswick-launch.co.uk) depart from the shore in Keswick.* The *Marina* (U E3) (🗺 e3) (*boats from £9/hour | Portinscale | tel. 017687 729 12 | www. derwentwatermarina.co.uk*) has all kinds of boats for hire, from stand-up paddleboards to rowing boats to motor boats. On the west side of the lake, the *Newland Activity Centre* (0) (🗺 0) (*Stair | Keswick | tel. 017687 784 63 | www.activity-centre. com*) offers a wide range of activities such as climbing, kayaking and archery.

WHERE TO STAY

KESWICK COUNTRY HOUSE HOTEL (U F1) (🗺 f1)
You'll feel like the lord of the manor in this elegant, modernised country-house hotel on the outskirts of Keswick. All you have to do is check in and enjoy yourself. *72 rooms | Station Road | tel. 08448 115585 | www.thekeswickhotel. co.uk | Expensive*

SEVEN OAKS GUEST HOUSE (U F2) (🗺 f2)
Fancy being part of the family? This small guesthouse has pretty rooms, a good breakfast and lovely people. *5 rooms | Surcharge for single nights | 7 Acorn*

There's always time for a little stroll along the Main Street in Keswick

Street | tel. 017687 7 20 88 | www.seven oaks-keswick.co.uk | *Budget*

Tourist Information Centre (U E1) (*∅ e1*) | 50 Main Street | tel. 017687 7 57 38 | www. keswick.org

WHERE TO GO

BASSENTHWAITE LAKE
(121 D4–5) (*∅ D4*)

Bassenthwaite Lake is not only the northernmost lake in the Lake District, it is also one of the most tranquil. There are no major settlements nearby, as is the case with most of the other lakes in the region. There's something else that makes it special, too: Bassenthwaite Lake is the only lake in the Lake District that has the word Lake in its name. The wonderful stately home *Mirehouse (April–Oct gardens daily* from *10am–3pm, house Wed, Sat/Sun 1.30pm–4pm | admission £7.80, garden only £4 | A591 | www.mirehouse.co.uk)* in the south east is well worth a visit. The completely furnished house contains many rare items of furniture, and some of the trees in the grounds are hundreds of years old.

A few years ago, at the north of Bassenthwaite Lake, a Scottish entrepreneur opened the ★ ● *Lakes Distillery (daily from 10am–5pm | tour £12.5£ | tel. 017687 8 88 50 | www.lakesdistillery. com)* which first sold only gin, vodka and whisky, but now also has the region's first Single Malt in its range. There is an extremely varied guided tour of the distillery – followed by a tasting hour. There is also a renowned restaurant on the premises, the *Bistro at the Distillery (www.bistroatthedistillery.com | Expensive)* that serves modern British cuisine with plenty of fresh fish as well as delicious home-made cakes.

Came here from Scotland: Bowder Stone at Borrowdale

BORROWDALE (121 D–E6) (🛱 D5)

In summer, Borrowdale to the south of Derwent Water is a brilliant green. The grass glows in the sun with the hills, which are covered in yew trees and oaks, forming a delightful contrast. Copper and graphite used to be mined here, charcoal burnt, and iron smelted. All that was long ago, and today Borrowdale lives mainly from tourism.

A good starting point is the car park at King's How between the two little towns of *Grange* and *Rosthwaite* with their pretty slate houses. You can walk the short distance to ☀ *Bowder Stone* a 9 m/29.5 ft high boulder that came originally from Scotland, and must have been pushed here by glaciers during the Ice Age. Sounds boring? There's a ladder to help you climb up – and the views are all the reward you need! ☀ *King's*

How and *Castle Crag* close by offer fabulous views of the valley. The almost 350-year-old stone bridge in Grange is a popular photo spot.

Good, plain British cuisine at *Stonethwaite's Langstrath Country Inn (8 rooms | 6 Chapel Howe | tel. 017687 7 72 39 | www. thelangstrath.co.uk | Moderate)*, which also has accommodation.

CASTLERIGG STONE CIRCLE ★ ☀ (121 E5) (🛱 D4)

Although it's only one of several hundred stone circles on the British Isles, it's a very special one: the smaller size may make the 40 stones of Castlerigg less impressive than, for instance, Stonehenge in the south of England. However, they are surrounded by an unforgettable mountain panorama that many in the south of the country eye with envy. If you come INSIDER TIP shortly after sunrise or just before sunset the colours are not only more vibrant for photographs, but there are fewer people around too. *Always accessible | admission free | Castle Lane | Underskiddaw | Keswick | www.english-heritage.org.uk*

ST JOHN'S IN THE VALE ☆
(121 E5–6) (Ⅲ D–E 4–5)

From this pretty valley you can see some of the most beautiful mountains of the Lake District. It is named after a small church, which was built back in the 19th century. Do take a look at the altar inside, which was designed by the great British architect Sir George Gilbert Scott – it was originally intended for a church in Keswick. There are some excellent photo spots in the area, and of course beautiful countryside everywhere.

THRELKELD QUARRY AND MINING MUSEUM ☆ (121 E5) (Ⅲ E4)

Granite was mined here for a little over a century, until it was no longer economically viable. What remains is quite spooky: the former mine was turned into a museum, where the quietly rusting machinery transports you back to days gone by. A small exhibition provides detailed information on granite mining, and you can go on an underground tour of a real mine. Three times a day, a quarry railway travels a short distance across the site. All in all, the museum is a big historic playground for adults, with excellent views of this corner of the Lake District. From Keswick there is INSIDER TIP a lovely footpath along a former rail track to Threlkeld; it starts on Station Road near Keswick Museum. *May–Oct daily from 10am–5pm | admission £3, tours £5 | Threlkeld Quarry | www.threlkeldquarryandmining museum.co.uk*

WHITEHAVEN

(120 A–B6) (Ⅲ A–B5) The age of the big cargo vessels may be over, but this port is always busy. There is also a touch of the maritime about the centre of Whitehaven (pop. 24,000) and its many shops.

The vast port was updated several years ago, and there are now plenty of restaurants and cafés.

There is a rather dainty lighthouse at the entrance, marking what was once the gateway for trade in Cumbria. Since the 18th century, the main imports were rum, tobacco and spices, which resulted in Whitehaven having a period as one of the biggest ports in Great Britain. However, those days are long gone, and today the boats that rock in the harbour basin are mainly yachts and smaller vessels. The *Candlestick Pit*, which soars up on the south west side, is a memorial to the mining days. This stone chimney was once part of a mine that closed in the 19th century.

SIGHTSEEING

BEACON MUSEUM

A large museum of local history in the port – and a very good one, too. The Beacon provides interesting information on the development of the region, from the time of Roman occupation and the long era of trade and mining, to the present. Children will particularly appreciate the museum as there is far more to see than to read, and special workshops ensure additional entertainment. And equally important, there are lovely views of the harbour from the top! *Tue–Sun 10am–4.30pm | admission £5.50 | West Strand | www.thebeacon-whitehaven.co.uk*

RUM STORY
Located in an original 1785 trading shop and warehouses, this museum tells a vivid story of when Whitehaven was a major importer of Caribbean rum. The tradition-steeped Jefferson family originally used the building to store wine and rum, which the museum illustrates quite realistically. The exhibits reflect several scenes that will also give children an impression of the life and trading activities in days gone by. *Mon–Sat 10am–4.30pm | admission £5.95 | 27 Lowther Street | www.rumstory.co.uk*

THE WATERFRONT ⊙
Dine like a captain: this excellent little restaurant in the harbour serves seasonal British dishes ranging from steak to fish. Almost all the produce come from the region. *West Strand | tel. 01946 32 81 84 | www.waterfrontwhitehaven.co.uk | Expensive*

ZEST HARBOURSIDE
Trendy, chic and right on the harbour: this is a branch of the restaurant in town serving burgers and meat as well as a good selection of vegetarian dishes. *Harbourside West Strand | tel. 01946 6 69 81 | www.zestwhitehaven.com | Moderate*

WHERE TO STAY

GEORGIAN HOUSE
Pretty rooms and a good restaurant with excellent British cuisine – this older, largely renovated hotel, situated right in the city centre, offers both. *8 rooms | 9–11 Church Street | tel. 01946 69 66 11 | www.georgianhousewhitehaven.co.uk | Moderate*

MORESBY HALL
You can sleep in a four-poster bed in this listed building just outside Whitehaven! *12 rooms | Moresby | tel. 01946 69 63 17 | www.moresbyhall.co.uk | Moderate*

INFORMATION

Tourist Information Centre | *Market Hall | Market Place | tel. 01946 59 89 14 | www.visit-whitehaven.co.uk*

WHERE TO GO

ENNERDALE WATER ★ (120 C6) *(f C5)*
The most westerly lake in the Lake District is also the least well-known and most original: only parts of Ennerdale Water have a road, and the paths around it are not as well developed as elsewhere. Since Ennerdale Valley was extensively reforested with spruce in the 20th century, the National Park authorities are now deliberately leaving it alone. This has created a rugged landscape which is no longer that evident in other parts of the Lake District.

Ennerdale Bridge, about 2 km/1.2 mi to the west, is a simple village (pop. 220) that has two pubs serving good food and overnight accommodation: *Shepherds Arms (8 rooms | Kirkland Road | tel. 01946 86 12 49 | www.shepherdsarms.com | Moderate) and the slightly more basic Fox & Hounds Inn (3 rooms | Ennerdale Bridge | Cleator | tel. 01946 86 13 73 | www.foxandhoundsinn.org | Moderate).*

MARYPORT (120 B4) *(𝄞 B3)*
The most notable aspect in the centre of this coastal town (pop. 11,000) is the layout. Terraced cottages were built in a special grid system during a period of extreme wealth: although the Romans built a port here in the 1st century, the

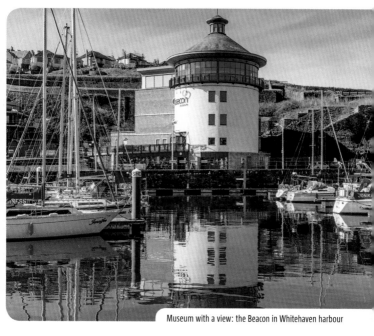

Museum with a view: the Beacon in Whitehaven harbour

Maryport of today mostly developed in the 19th century. Wealthy businessmen from the Lake District needed a port to export their goods; Maryport was easy to get to, and therefore perfect for their causes. In the meantime, though, the town has become something of a dormitory – a lot of people live here but work elsewhere.

What remains is the very pretty coast – and its Roman heritage in the form of stones and sculptures at the ★ Senhouse Roman Museum (April–Oct daily 10am–5pm, Nov–March Fri–Sun 10.30am–4pm | admission £4 | The Battery | Sea Brows | www.senhousemuseum.co.uk). Most of the exhibits were obtained in an archaeological dig at a former Roman site in the field adjacent to the museum. There is an excellent view over this impressive site from a tower at the main entrance.

The Maryport Maritime Museum (April–Oct Tue, Thu–Sun 10.30am–5pm, Nov–March 10.30am–4pm | admission £3 | 1 Senhouse Street | www.maryportmaritimemuseum.com) has collected paintings and other exhibits to illustrate how the town developed from a tiny Roman port to the gateway to Cumbria in the 19th century. Thomas Henry Ismay, founder of the White Star Line shipping company, famous for the Titanic, was born in Maryport. A separate area is dedicated to him.

From the a INSIDER TIP Harbourside Café (South Quay | tel. 01900 817760 | www.coastaquarium.co.uk | Budget) in the Coast Aquarium there is a good view of the harbour, which can be enjoyed alongside delicious cakes and tasty snacks. The Ellenbank Hotel (26 rooms | Birkby | tel. 01900 815233 | www.ellen

bank.co.uk | Moderate) couldn't be more British – simple, homely rooms in an old Victorian building just outside the town. Information: *Tourist Information Centre | Irish Street | tel. 01900 811450*

ST BEES (124 A1) *(ᗰ A–B5)*

Before the invention of GPS, this was how sailors were able to navigate their way through this part of the Irish Sea: the ⚡ *Lighthouse* of St Bees (7 km/ 4.4 mi south of Whitehaven). Today it is the destination of a lovely, approximately 6 km/3.7 mi walk starting from the beach in the town (pop. 1800). You can swim in the sandy areas but don't get too close to the rocky coast, as there are countless rocks underwater that make it very dangerous. Not far from the lighthouse is an old foghorn station, but neither are open to visitors. If you want to walk for much longer, set off from here on the Coast-to-Coast Walk, which runs across the Yorkshire Dales some 300 km/186 mi to North Yorkshire on the east coast of England.

St Bees School, founded in 1583, is an exceptional Elizabethan building in the middle of the town and one of England's

LIE TO ME

Even children are taught not to lie. But once a year in the Lake District the cry goes up: Lie to me! Every November, the *Bridge Inn* in Santon Bridge hosts the competition to find the biggest liar in the world. The competitors each have five minutes to tell the jury the tallest tales they know. There is a historic background to this unusual competition. In the 18th century, Will Ritson was a highly-regarded man in Wasdale – although even then he was well-known for telling porkies, or tall tales. For instance, he claimed that the turnips in the dale grew so large that families quarried them to use them as byres or barns for the sheep. On another occasion, he claimed to have crossed a golden eagle with a foxhound to breed dogs with wings to fly. What is an undeniable truth: he became the model for the self-declared biggest liar competition in the world.

Fresh breeze on the Irish Sea – the beach at St Bees

historic schools. You'll find basic rooms at the *Manor Hotel (7 rooms | 11–12 Main Street | tel. 01946 82 05 87 | Budget)* next to the station. Good British food is served in the adjacent pub *(Moderate)*.

WORKINGTON (120 B5) *(ፙ B4)*

The harbour town of Workington (pop. 24,000) has little in the way of sights to attract visitors, but is excellent for shopping. The usual town centre shops can be found between Oxford Street and Pow Street, as well as a real department store – not an everyday sight in the Lake District. Close to the town centre are the ruins of Workington Hall (Ladies' Walk), sometimes called Curwen Hall. The once opulent manor house is now freely accessible, and occasionally a concert venue in summer. To give you an impression of what it used to look like, there is a model in the *Helena Thompson Museum (Mon–Fri 10am–4.30pm, Sun 1.30pm–4.30pm | admission free | Park End Road | www.helenathompson.org.uk)*, an elegant Georgian house that is dedicated to the 19th century.

Good British pub food ranging from burgers to fish & chips are served at the *Henry Bessemer (New Oxford Street | tel. 01900 73 46 50 | Budget)*. The *Sleepwell Inn* in the town centre *(27 rooms | Washington Street | tel. 01900 6 57 72 | www.washingtoncentralhotel.co.uk/sleepwell | Budget)* has plain but modern rooms.

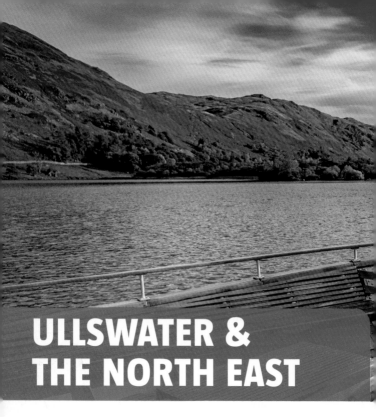

ULLSWATER & THE NORTH EAST

The north east of the Lake District is a popular destination for people who want to explore the National Park in a more relaxing way.

The area includes Ullswater, the second-largest lake in the National Park and one of the most popular. Due to the slightly higher than average age of its visitors, it is occasionally referred to as the "pensioners' lake", but please don't let that put you off. The world-famous *Ullswater Steamers*, 150-year-old excursion boats, putter up and down the lake, which is surrounded by mountains, all year round (except on 24/25 December). There are many walking trails, the best-known being Ullswater Way, a circular route around the lake. Parts of the old Roman road can still be seen on the south shore. The breathtaking mountain landscape of Kirkstone Pass links the area to Windermere and Ambleside. Penrith, by contrast, which is east of Ullswater and just outside the Lake District, is a small town with a pedestrian zone and lots of shops and has long been the most important business centre in the region.

Something that people in Shap a little further to the south, eye with envy: the once extremely busy market town has become much quieter since the construction of the M6, the much frequented north/south motorway. However, even today this is still the best place to get to the east of the Lake District , parts of which would otherwise not be accessible by car.

Even the Romans were attracted to this area – and nowadays Ullswater is still a popular destination for boat rides and walking tours

PENRITH

(122–123 C–D 4–5) (🕮 F4) **Other places in the Lake District may have mountain views and lake access, but Penrith (pop. 15,000) has its town centre.**
The centre has developed around the old clock tower on the *Market Square,* with lots of shops, pubs and restaurants. The Georgian architecture has largely been retained, which gives the town an extremely authentic feel – alt-

hough this is also partly due to the fact that many of the buildings have not been updated for some time. An extension to the town centre has been developed to the south, the New Squares. There is not much life here yet, apart from a large supermarket and a hotel. Nontheless, the architecture is a success. Penrith may not be the prettiest town in Cumbria, but it is one of the main centres. It is certainly the perfect starting point for exploring the north of the Lake District.

SIGHTSEEING

BROUGHAM CASTLE ★

The old castle ruin on the Eamont River, a short distance from the centre, is as idyllic as a picture postcard. Most of the external walls are still standing, and you are welcome to walk around freely – and join the few dozen sheep doing the same. A small exhibition at the entrance tells its history. Brougham Castle dates back

Relax in style at
The George Hotel in Penrith

to the 13th century, and was of strategic importance due to its proximity to Scotland. It was abandoned in the 17th century. *April–Sept daily from 10am–6pm, Oct 10am–4pm, Nov–March Sat/Sun 10am–4pm | admission £4.90 | Moor Lane | www.english-heritage.org.uk*

KING ARTHUR'S ROUND TABLE

It has not been proven that this Neolithic henge really is the spot where King Arthur's Knights of the Round Table gathered, but it's still an exciting prehistoric circular earthwork. On the other side, a short distance from the town, lies Mayburgh Henge, a much bigger hill with a menhir, a tall upright stone. *Always accessible | admission free | Eamont Bridge | B5320 | www.english-heritage.org.uk*

PENRITH CASTLE

Not much is left of Penrith Castle, a castle built of red stone, but the walls that are still standing are impressive. The Duke of Gloucester lived here for a few years before he was crowned King Richard III. *Always accessible | admission free | Ullswater Road | www.english-heritage.org.uk*

FOOD & DRINK

THE DOG BECK

A good example of a centuries-old pub with a modern interior. The inside has been completely refurbished, and it now serves a wide selection of beers, gins and pub food ranging from burgers to wraps, as well as vegetarian dishes. From 7am there is an INSIDER TIP extensive breakfast menu. *20–22 Southend Road | tel. 01768 84 04 91 | www.jdwetherspoon.com | Budget*

RAJ 🌿

The sheer number of vegetarian dishes on the menu at this Indian restaurant are a reminder that many Indians don't eat any meat at all. The food is not only hot and spicy, but also – unlike many Indian restaurants elsewhere – pretty authentic. *17–18 King Street | tel. 01768 89 25 74 | Moderate*

SHOPPING

Penrith may have three large super-markets, more than other towns in the Lake District, but more noteworthy are the many independent shops. INSIDER TIP *James and John Graham (6–7 Market Square | www.jjgraham. co.uk)* is a well-stocked delicatessen with lots of local products. The old estate of *Old Brougham Hall (Brougham | www.broughamhall.co.uk)* a short distance from the town centre has been turned into a craft centre with lots of arty shops.

LEISURE & SPORTS

The C2C Cycle Route *(www.c2c-guide. co.uk)* which connects the east coast at Tynemouth with Whitehaven in Cumbria (225 km/140 mi away) runs through Penrith – as a result, the town caters for cyclists with cycle paths and safe places to leave bikes. Bikes can be hired from I*nspiring Cycling (from £25/day including delivery | tel. 07887 76 49 87 | www.inspi ringcycling.co.uk).*

ENTERTAINMENT

Penrith was renowned for its many breweries and pubs. Nowadays the nightlife still revolves around the remaining pubs. The Warehouse (43 Burrowgate) has the usual drinks plus karaoke, while the Alhambra (47 Middlegate) has a small cinema.

WHERE TO STAY

THE GEORGE HOTEL

A traditional hotel in the centre that is excellent for a relaxing stay – with well-furnished rooms, an elegant restaurant *(Moderate)* and a cosy bar. *35 rooms |* Devonshire Street | tel. 01768 86 26 96 | www.lakedistricthotels.net | *Moderate*

NORTH LAKES HOTEL

Don't pay too much attention to the location of this hotel (near the motorway exit), but focus on what lies within: modern rooms, a spa and pool. *8 rooms | Ullswater Road | tel. 01768 86 8111 | www.thwaites.co.uk/hotels-and-inns | Expensive*

INFORMATION

Tourist Information Centre | 42 Middle-gate | tel. 01768 86 74 66 | www.disco verpenrith.co.uk

MARCO POLO HIGHLIGHTS

⭐ **Ullswater Steamers**
Put your feet up and relax – on a boat trip around Ullswater!
→ p. 85

⭐ **Kirkstone Pass**
Here's to the view – which is perfect over a pint outside the Kirkstone Inn → p. 86

⭐ **Brougham Castle**
Don't forget your camera: these castle ruins in Penrith seem like they were built to look like this → p. 78

⭐ **Carlisle Cathedral**
Unusual in England: Carlisle's cathedral is made entirely out of red sandstone → p. 80

⭐ **Lowther Castle**
Although only the walls remain of this castle, they are so impressive that you don't actually miss anything else → p. 81

WHERE TO GO

ACORN BANK (123 E5) *(ᛗ G4)*

All show and no substance? Acorn Bank (12 km/7.5 mi east of Penrith) is a romantic red, ivy-clad mansion that is in a permanent state of restoration, which means it is only sparsely furnished, some areas without wallpaper, but it is open to visitors. Yet perhaps this is what makes it so charming. It means you can focus entirely on the architecture, the stucco ceilings and creaking wood floors, and constantly discover new things. The garden is notable in particular for several hundred herbs (the National Trust's largest collection of medicinal and culinary plants), and various rare orchids that you wouldn't expect to see at these latitudes. It's a short walk to the working water mill that is still used to produce the flour used in the shop and tea room. The mansion also has a holiday apartment *(tel. 01225 79 22 74 | www.nationaltrust.org.uk/holidays | Expensive) to rent. April–Oct Wed–Mon 10am–5pm, Nov–March Sat/Sun 10am–4pm | admission £7 | Temple Sowerby | www.nationaltrust.org.uk*

CALDBECK (122 A3) *(ᛗ E3)*

The most northerly town (pop. 730) in the Lake District is also one of the most idyllic. There are cream-coloured terraced houses, the box trees are neatly trimmed, and Whelpo Beck flows alongside them through the village. It's so pretty that it should be on a picture postcard. The ◉ *Watermill Café (Priest's Mill | tel. 016974 7 82 67 | www.watermillcafe.co.uk | Budget)* in an old water mill next to the church serves tasty treats. *Glebe Cottage (Old Rectory | tel. 016974 7 84 84 | Moderate)*, also next to the church, is a comfortable self-catering holiday let. *Information: www.caldbeckvillage.co.uk*

CARLISLE (122 B1–2) *(ᛗ E1)*

At first, Cumbria's capital (pop. 75,000), looks about as rough as the weather in the county. However, once you engage with the town, you'll soon discover one of its many pretty corners. The town centre around the Market Cross monument is surrounded by lovely old buildings and branches of every conceivable retail chain.

The ★ ● *Carlisle Cathedral (Mon–Sat 7.30am–6.15pm, Sun until 5pm | admission free | Castle Street | www.carlisle cathedral.org.uk)* from the 12th century is one of the few British cathedrals to have been built in red sandstone. Although it is the second smallest one on the

LOW BUDGET

It's usually the evening meal that is most expensive in the Lake District. If you want to save a little money, eat out at lunchtime – or do as the locals do and head to the fish & chip shop. You can usually get a decent portion of deep-fried fish fillet and chunky chips for about £4–5 – and don't forget malt vinegar and lots of salt. *Angel Lane Chippie (17 Angel Lane)* in Penrith is a popular address for them.

Cocktails are becoming increasingly popular in ordinary pubs although they're not always cheap. You can save, for instance, in Penrith if you go to the Happy Hour at *Foundry Thirty Four (34 Burrowgate | Sandgate)*, a restaurant with a bar that offers all cocktails at half-price from Sun–Fri 5pm–6.30pm. Meals are also served at half-price then too!

Picture postcard: Caldbeck is the most northerly village in the Lake District

island, it is most impressive on the inside. Its attractions include the east window in coloured glass with scenes from the Bible. When the sun shines through it, the gloomy, cool interior of the building is bathed in delightful colours. The treasury in the underground vault contains excavated items, valuable goblets and other items collected by former bishops. *Carlisle Castle (April–Sept daily from 10am–6pm, Oct 10am–5pm, Nov–March Sat/Sun 10am–4pm | admission £6.80 | Castle Way | www.english-heritage.org.uk)* on the outskirts of the town centre is a 900-year-old large, completely preserved castle. Because of its proximity to the border with Scotland, it used to be of military significance, as is highlighted in the integrated military museum. Mary, Queen of Scots was once imprisoned here. A ⚜ tower has been named after her, from which you can enjoy

a good view over the rooftops of Carlisle. Excellent coffee and cakes are available in the delightfully old-fashioned café INSIDERTIP ► *John Watt & Son (11 Bank Street | www.johnwattandson.co.uk)*. The Halston Aparthotel *(16 rooms | 20–34 Warwick Road | tel. 01228 21 02 40 | www.thehalston.com | Moderate)* has modern self-catering apartments with a good restaurant (British cuisine, *Expensive*) and hotel facilities.

LOWTHER CASTLE ★ (123 D5) (*⑭ F4*)
Even close up it is hard to see that nowadays all that remains of this impressive castle are the walls. Lowther Castle is a 17th century country house that was built with an almost wasteful abundance of fortified walls and towers. Despite the lack of ceilings and roofs, it is still as impressive as ever. It stands on the edge of what was once a carefully cultivated

As idyllic as a natural lake – although Haweswater was dammed artificially

extensive garden. Work has been underway for a number of years now to restore it in small sections. The castle roof was removed in the 1950s, leaving the building exposed to the elements and thus destruction. At least the owners, who were no longer able to maintain it, managed to avoid taxation.

Nearby Askham Hall (13 rooms | Askham | tel. 01931 712350 | www.askhamhall. co.uk | Expensive), is still habitable, and now an elegant hotel with a beautiful gardens. On the other side of the M6, not far from Lowther is the INSIDER TIP *Abbott Lodge (Clifton | www.abbottlodge jerseyicecream.co.uk)* dairy, which produces and sells delicious ice cream made from Jersey cows' milk. Lowther *Castle April–Sept daily from 10am–5pm, otherwise until 4pm | admission £9 | Lowther | www.lowthercastle.org*

SHAP

(123 D6) *(⌘ G5)* **Two long lines of grey stone houses, many dating from the 18th century, frame the main road in Shap (pop. 1200). Once upon a time this road used to be the main connection between England and Scotland.**

The motorway was built years ago and the town is much quieter now. It lives from tourism thanks to its proximity to the eastern side of the Lake District. You can only get to places like Haweswater from this side, and not directly from the National Park. The Yorkshire Dales, in the east, is the next National Park and no less attractive.

Shap Summit, a good 3 km/1.9 mi south of the town, is a place of pilgrimage for railway fans. At 278 m/912 ft, this mountain pass is the highest point on the west coast route between London and Glasgow. Many people come here only to take a selfie in front of the sign. Shap is also known for its blue and pink granite that is still mined here today.

SIGHTSEEING

KELD CHAPEL
The medieval chapel in this extremely rural part of Shap is easy to miss. Made of loose stones, the building is believed to have once been part of the nearby Abbey. The unusual simplicity of the inside of the chapel with plain wooden benches and a table as the altar is of particular appeal. *Always accessible (key is at the Taylors' house opposite) | admission free | Keld Lane | www.natio naltrust.org.uk*

SHAP ABBEY
An unusual spot for the remains of a once magnificent Abbey. There is now a farmhouse on the site where Shap Abbey once stood, and parts of it have been integrated in the farm. The most visible signs of the complex, which was built in the early 13th century, are the ruins of the west tower. It is open to visitors and various foundation walls can also be viewed. Shap Abbey was the last Abbey to be founded in England. Many of the stones that are now missing were used in the construction of Shap market hall and Lowther Castle near Penrith. *Always accessible | admission free | www. english-heritage.org.uk*

FOOD & DRINK

SHAP CHIPPY
Everything is freshly prepared in this award-winning fish and chips restaurant – great food to take away or eat in.

It can get busy at times so it's advisable to book ahead to avoid disappointment. *Main Street | tel. 01931 71 60 60 | www.shapchippy.co.uk | Budget*

WHERE TO STAY

SHAP WELLS HOTEL
A thermal spa under the hotel used to attract celebrities, but today it is a comfortable country hotel in a peaceful setting. The spring is no longer in use. *98 rooms | B6261 | tel. 01931 71 66 28 | www.shap wells.com | Moderate*

INFORMATION

Information Point | *The Old Courthouse | Main Street | tel. 01931 71 75 39*

WHERE TO GO

HAWESWATER (122 C6) (*∅ F5*)
This artificial lake was created at the end of the 1930s by damming two natural lakes, High Water and Low Water to supply water to the Greater Manchester area. The two villages of Measand and Mardale Green were flooded by the new reservoir, and lost. Visitors often have the lake to themselves. As it is only accessible by car from the east, few tourists find themselves heading in this direction. This is what makes Haweswater so special.
You can't get right onto the shore, but from Mardale Green car park, at the end of the only access road, there is a 14 km/ 8.7 mi trail around the lake. If you want something a little more strenuous, you can head west from the same car park, past Small Water to the top of the High Street, and then walk back in an arch (9.5 km/5.9 mi with several ascents). The isolated but comfortable and beautifully refurbished ☆ *Haweswater Hotel*

(17 rooms | Lakeside Road | Bampton | tel. 01931 713235 | www.haweswater hotel.com | Expensive) is the only place to eat and sleep. It has wonderful views of the lake.

ULLSWATER

(122 B–C 5–6) (Ø E–F 4–5) **A few small towns and villages breathe life into Ullswater in the north east of the Lake District without it being as overrun as other lakes.**

Glenridding (pop. 500) is the best starting point to explore the lake shore as the village offers direct access. There are boats all year round. You probably won't notice, but this used to be an important mining village.

Pooley Bridge (pop. 300) in the east is named after an old bridge washed away by a flood. You can easily relax in this pretty village – join everyone else sitting outside one of the pubs or cafés on a sunny day and watch the world go by. Between April and September on the last Sunday of the month (10.30am–2.30pm) there is INSIDER TIP one of the best farmers' markets in the whole of Cumbria.

SIGHTSEEING

AIRA FORCE

Surrounded by dense woodlands, Aira Force, the most beautiful waterfall in the Lake District, plunges down 20 m/ 65.6 ft. From the car park, it's a good 15-minute walk over uneven ground. You'll have the best view of the waterfall from the lower of two stone bridges. You'll see plenty of red squirrels that are typical of this area, especially in the morning and evening. You can enjoy an afternoon cuppa in peace at the Tea Room *(Budget)* in the car park. *Always accessible | admission free | A592 (corner Park Brow) | www.nationaltrust.org.uk*

COCKPIT STONE CIRCLE ☼

This stone circle near Pooley Bridge can only be reached on foot (straight on along the High Street). Because of the small stones it looks quite unassuming, but the surroundings more than compensate for that. Cockpit stands high above Ullswater with views of the distant Derwent Fells. *Always accessible | admission free | High Street extension*

GREENSIDE MINE

The Glenridding Beck meanders along against the backdrop of the sparse peaks of the surrounding mountains – while there's an enviable stillness in the old granite building which was once one of the biggest lead mines in the United Kingdom. The site of Greenside Mine is a wonderful relic from bygone days. One part contains a tranquil INSIDER TIP youth hostel *(18 multi-bed rooms | tel. 0345 3 71 97 42 (*) | www.yha.org.uk/hos tel/yha-helvellyn | Budget)* where guests find complete peace.

The mine itself is not open to visitors. In the 1960s, it was used as one of the sites in Operation Orpheus. This was the code name under which the UK Atomic Weapons Research Establishment carried out underground atomic explosions. However, the authorities assure us that everything above ground has long been safe. There is a narrow, approximately 2-km/1.2-mi long path along Glenridding Beck from the town to the mine.

FOOD & DRINK

BECKSIDE BAR

The lovely Glenridding Hotel (36 rooms) is also home to this excellent, modern bar offering tasty small dishes (British cuisine), everything is beautifully prepared and presented. *A592 | Glenridding | tel. 017684 8 22 28 | www.theglenridding hotel.com | Expensive*

GRANNY DOWBEKIN'S TEAROOMS

You'll find the perfect place to refuel right next to the bridge: delicious cakes and fabulous sandwiches, all made locally. There are also vegan and gluten-free options. You can sit outside in the small garden. *Pooley Bridge | tel. 017684 8 64 53 | www.grannydowbekins.co.uk | Budget*

LEISURE & SPORTS

From the jetty in Glenridding and Pooley Bridge the ✹ ★ *Ullswater Steamers (day ticket £14.20 | Glenridding Pier House | tel. 017684 8 22 29 | www.ullswater-steamers.co.uk)* shuttle across the lake several times a day.

St Patrick's Boat Landing (Grisedale Bridge | Glenridding | tel. 017684 8 23 93 | www.stpatricksboatlandings. co.uk) hires out bikes, rowing and motor boats. Boats are also available at *Lakeland Boat Hire (Rivermouth | Eusemere | Pooley Bridge | tel. 017684 8 68 00 | www.lakelandboathire.co.uk) (all from £16 an hour).*

By far the most popular walk is about 14 km/8.7 mi long, and runs west from Glenridding right up Helvellyn, the third-highest mountain in England. By contrast, the 32 km/19.9 mi long Ullswater Way *(www.ullswater.com/the-ulls water-way)* takes you around the lake through wonderful countryside and some of the larger towns. Wherever you look, there are wonderful views. The walk also passes all four jetties. The path is indicated by a circular logo with a yellow flower.

For the old steamers on Ullswater, the journey alone is a reward

ULLSWATER

WHERE TO STAY

ANOTHER PLACE ● ∿

This unique and amazing hotel connects you with the elements with no compromise on style or comfort. Situated right next to the lake in 18 acres of Lake District National Park. Every room is a place of relaxation with fabulous views of the surrounding area; there is also a large spa. *40 rooms | Watermillock | tel. 01768 48 64 42 | www.another.place | Expensive*

INN ON THE LAKE

Something for a very special holiday: this lovely Victorian hotel is right next to Ullswater. Traditional rooms, ∿ INSIDER TIP a very good afternoon tea with views of the lake, and an excellent restaurant *(Expensive)*, also open to non-residents. *47 rooms | Glenridding | tel. 0800 8 40 12 45 | www.lakedistricthotels.net | Expensive*

INFORMATION

Ullswater Information Centre | Beckside Car Park | tel. 017684 8 24 12 | www.lakedistrict.gov.uk

WHERE TO GO

DALEMAIN (122 C5) *(ௐ F4)*

Not quite as impressive as Downton Abbey in the eponymous TV series, but much cosier: this medieval estate has consistently been extended and is still inhabited. It is the home of the Hasell-McCosh family, who are happy to offer groups of visitors guided tours of their home which is full of fine furniture, porcelain, toys and family portraits. And they'll happily talk about the building's special features and its occupants – and the priest's hiding place. The customary cream tea is available in the adjacent Tea Room *(Budget)*, there is also a large garden behind the main building. *Dalemain Estate | April–Oct Sun–Thu 10.30am–3.30pm | admission £11.50 (garden only £8.50) | www.dalemain.com*

KIRKSTONE PASS ★ ● ∿
(125 F1) *(ௐ E6)*

Even if narrow, steep roads fill you with dread, the drive up Kirkstone Pass (A592), which connects Ullswater with Windermere, is one of the highlights of the Lake District. The mountain road is up to 454 m/1,490 ft high, and follows a fabulous mountain landscape with moss

FOR BOOKWORMS

Believing the Lie – (2012) This thriller by Elizabeth George is about an influential family in the Lake District. A murder turns its tranquil life upside down. Inspector Lynley solves the case – exciting if you like whodunnits

The Shepherd's Life – (2016) A book that gives an in-depth impression of life in the Lake District. Writer James Rebanks describes his own personal view of his family's deep roots as shepherds in the mountains. You'll learn a lot about the daily working life, nature and the landscape – and not least, of course, about the Herdwick sheep who live in various parts of the National Park

Breathtaking isolation: there are steep roads up to Kirkstone Pass

and grass-covered slopes, past sleepy sheep and isolated trails.

At a height of 451 m/1,480 ft is the Kirkstone Inn *(tel. 015394 3 38 88 | www. kirkstonepassinn.com | Budget)*, not only one of the oldest pubs in England (built in 1496), but also the third highest. You can enjoy a pint of exclusive beer here: INSIDER TIP *Kirkstone* is only brewed for this pub. There is also rustic pub food, including one of the best coleslaws in England. There are also four very basic B&B rooms above the bar *(Budget)*.

PATTERDALE (122 B6) *(ɯ E5)*

This is the home of the Patterdale Terrier, a highly energetic and intelligent breed. The town (pop. 500) benefits from a youth hostel, a car park and the surrounding area. Nestled in the valley on the south end of the lake, Patterdale is a slightly less expensive alternative for exploring Ullswater than the hotels right on the water. Walkers in particular appreciate the many options for tours in the surrounding mountains.

The rooms in the *Patterdale Hotel (57 rooms | A592 | tel. 017684 8 22 31 | www.patterdalehotel.co.uk | Expensive)* are comfortable without being fussy, and guests have the added benefit of being able to park their cars here free of charge. Otherwise parking on the village's second official car park can get expensive. The *White Lion Inn (A592 | tel. 017684 8 22 14 | Moderate)* is a very nice pub with good British food, traditional beers and a friendly atmosphere.

DISCOVERY TOURS

1

THE LAKE DISTRICT AT A GLANCE

START: ❶ Kendal
END: ㉖ Cartmel

10 days
Actual driving time
8–9 hours

Distance:
➡ approx. 500 km/310 mi

COSTS: approx. £1800 per person (for two people in a double room in a mid-range hotel) for accommodation, meals, admission charges, fuel

WHAT TO PACK: Comfortable and sturdy shoes, rain jacket, sunscreen in summer, jumpers in summer as well

IMPORTANT TIPS: ❷ Bowness-on-Windermere: Boat trip to Lakeside: Timetable at *www.windermere-lakecruises.co.uk*
㉕ Ulverston: Hoad Monument only open on Sundays

Would you like to explore the places that are unique to this region? Then the Discovery Tours are just the thing for you – they include terrific tips for stops worth making, breathtaking places to visit, selected restaurants and fun activities. It's even easier with the Touring App: download the tour with map and route to your smartphone using the QR Code on pages 2/3 or from the website address in the footer below – and you'll never get lost again even when you're offline.

TOURING APP

○

→ p. 2/3

Mountains, lakes and lots of little towns – this tour takes you around the key sights of the Lake District. You'll stop at the loveliest spots and experience the highlights of the National Park. The perfect route for a first visit.

Set off from ❶ Kendal → p. 47, the southern gateway to the Lake District. Enjoy a leisurely walk around the town, which has lots of shops, to the ruins of Kendal Castle (Parr Street). After lunch at the Globe Pub *(tel. 01539 72 18 52 | globekendal.co.uk | Moderate)* on Market Place, and **continue to** ❷ Bowness-on-Winder-

DAY 1
❶ Kendal
20 km/12.4 mi
❷ Bowness-on-Winder-mere

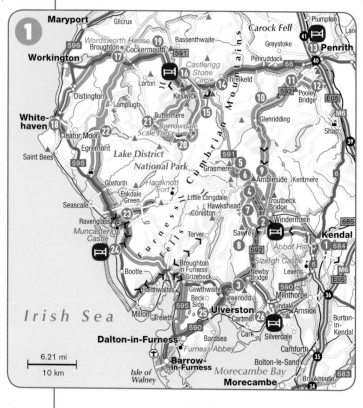

mere → p. 38. Wander through the tiny town centre to Lake Windermere. Fancy an ice cream? The INSIDER TIP **Windermere Ice Cream Company** (Chestnut Road) makes fabulous flavours! Spend the next three nights in Bowness, perhaps at the elegant, Laura Ashley-furnished The Belsfield.

Go to the supermarket for picnic supplies. At 10.30am, head to the pier at Bowness for a **boat trip to Lakeside → p. 40, where the historic steam train to ③ Haverthwaite** awaits. First, though, stop for a picnic. Take a look inside the Engine Shed, which has a number of old engines, before you **take the train back to Lakeside and the boat to ④** Ambleside → p. 33. Wind down with a cream tea at the Waterhead Hotel. **The no. 599 bus goes back to Bowness.**

DAY 2

19 km/11.8 mi

③ Haverthwaite

23 km/14.3 mi

④ Ambleside

DISCOVERY TOURS

In the morning, continue to ❺ Grasmere → p. 43. This picture perfect resort is also known for its delicious gingerbread. **Then go back to Rydal** and explore ❻ Rydal Mount → p. 47, for many years home to the poet William Wordsworth. **Now go to Ambleside and on to** ❼ Hawkshead → p. 36. You deserve a late lunch, perhaps at the King's Arms Hotel. Refreshed, have a look at the Beatrix Potter Gallery, which contains the drawings by the famous writer of children's books, and **on the way back see** ❽ Hill Top → p. 36, where she lived early in her life. **Take the ferry from the ferry terminal on Windermere and cross to Bowness.**

Head for Ambleside, but once out of Windermere turn onto the A592, which will take you to ❾ Kirkstone Pass → p. 86, one of the most impressive pass roads in England. Admire the views over a cup of tea at the Kirkstone Pass Inn! **This road will take you directly to** Ullswater → p. 84. **Stop about 4 km/2.5 mi past Glenridding at the** ❿ Aira Force Waterfalls → p. 84, which includes a short walk. **Next stop is** ⓫ Pooley Bridge → p. 85, where you can hire a rowing boat on the shore (past the bridge on the right). Enjoy the peace on the water before **heading on towards** Lowther. Although only the walls are left of ⓬ Lowther Castle → p. 81, a walk around it will show you just how impressive this building still is. **The A6 will take you to** ⓭ Penrith → p. 77, where you could perhaps spend the night at the George Hotel.

After breakfast, buy food for a picnic, ideally from Marks & Spencer (22–27 King Street), and set **off for Keswick. At Threlkeld, take the turning for** ⓮ Threlkeld Quarry and Mining Museum → p. 71. Go for a short ride over the site on the mine train. **Next stop is** ⓯ Castlerigg Stone Circle → p. 70, an old stone circle in a most impressive mountain setting. Time for your picnic! **Then go straight to** ⓰ Keswick → p. 67, where you can end the day with a performance at the Theatre by the Lake. You could find accommodation for the next three nights at somewhere like the Keswick Country House Hotel.

Depart for ⓱ Cockermouth → p. 64! Visit Wordsworth House and Garden, the birthplace of the poet William Wordsworth, which is right in the centre of the town. After tea in the café, enjoy a gentle walk around the

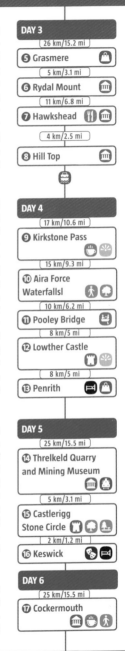

DAY 3
26 km/15.2 mi
❺ Grasmere
5 km/3.1 mi
❻ Rydal Mount
11 km/6.8 mi
❼ Hawkshead
4 km/2.5 mi
❽ Hill Top

DAY 4
17 km/10.6 mi
❾ Kirkstone Pass
15 km/9.3 mi
❿ Aira Force Waterfalls
10 km/6.2 mi
⓫ Pooley Bridge
8 km/5 mi
⓬ Lowther Castle
8 km/5 mi
⓭ Penrith

DAY 5
25 km/15.5 mi
⓮ Threlkeld Quarry and Mining Museum
5 km/3.1 mi
⓯ Castlerigg Stone Circle
2 km/1.2 mi
⓰ Keswick

DAY 6
25 km/15.5 mi
⓱ Cockermouth

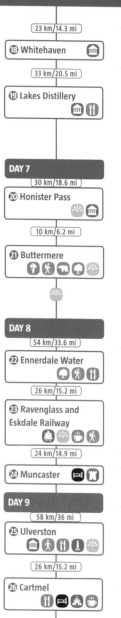

23 km/14.3 mi

⑱ Whitehaven 🏛

33 km/20.5 mi

⑲ Lakes Distillery 🏛 🍴

DAY 7

30 km/18.6 mi

⑳ Honister Pass ❋ 🏛

10 km/6.2 mi

㉑ Buttermere 🌳 🚶 🐑 🍵 ❋

❋

DAY 8

54 km/33.6 mi

㉒ Ennerdale Water 🍵 🚶 🍴

26 km/15.2 mi

㉓ Ravenglass and Eskdale Railway 🚂 ❋ 🍵 🚶

24 km/14.9 mi

㉔ Muncaster 🛏 🏰

DAY 9

58 km/36 mi

㉕ Ulverston 🏛 🚶 🍴 ℹ ❋

26 km/15.2 mi

㉖ Cartmel 🍴 🛏 🏠 🍵

town for a while before **driving on to ⑱** Whitehaven → p. 71. There, the Rum Story will take you back to the days when the town was one of the most important ports in the area. **On the way back to Keswick, take the turning at Bassenthwaite Lake → p. 69 to the ⑲** Lakes Distillery → p. 69. This restored distillery has been producing whisky, gin and vodka for a number of years. You'll find out how on a guided tour. The distillery restaurant is perfect for an evening meal.

Put on your sturdy footwear and **drive south-east to ⑳** Honister Pass → p. 63. The views on this mountain road are sensational after just the first one hundred metres! Stop at the top at the Honister Slate Mine. A guided tour will tell you all about slate mining in this area. **Afterwards drive on to ㉑** Buttermere → p. 61. Time for some home-made ice cream at the Syke Farm Tea Room. Then stroll past the curious sheep to Lake Buttermere, and walk once around it. Enjoy the views – although they are going to get even better. The drive back will take you **behind the church back to Keswick along a pass.**

Continue via Cockermouth to ㉒ Ennerdale Water → p. 72. Take advantage of this moderately-sized lake for a stroll along the beach. **In the neighbouring town of Ennerdale Bridge** you'll find plenty of places for lunch, such as The Gather *(tel. 01946 86 24 53 | thegatherennerdale. com | Budget)* before **continuing to** Ravenglass → p. 54. Park at the station, because **you'll be taking** the **㉓** Ravenglass and Eskdale Railway → p. 54 11 km/6.8 mi through this pretty part of the Lake District. At the end stop in Dalegarth for Boot, and treat yourself to a cuppa and a gentle stroll around before returning by train. **The last stop of the day is ㉔** Muncaster, where you will spend the night.

Before you leave, visit Muncaster Castle → p. 56. **Continue to ㉕** Ulverston → p. 57 and the Laurel & Hardy Museum. After a stroll through the town, head to The Farmers for some lunch, because you've still got quite a walk ahead of you: Ford Park takes you to the Hoad Monument on a hill. Although you can only visit it on Sundays, it's worth it for the views. **On to the final stage and ㉖** Cartmel → p. 41, where you can check in to the Priory Hotel. This is your last evening in the Lake District – enjoy it over an excellent meal at the award-winning restaurant L'Enclume.

Stroll through the town to Cartmel Priory. Directly opposite, you can see how cheese is made and beer brewed.
However, Cartmel is best-known for its sticky toffee pudding, which you can try in the café of the Village Shop.
See you again in the Lake District!

DAY 10

② AT THE HEART OF THE LAKE DISTRICT

START: ① Allan Bank, Grasmere END: ⑧ Baldry's Tea Room, Grasmere	6 hours Actual walking time 1½ hours
Distance: 🔘 approx. 5.5 km/3.4 mi	

COSTS: approx. £36 per person for meals and admission charges
WHAT TO PACK: Comfortable shoes, drinking water, rain jacket or
sunscreen depending on the weather

Wordsworth's writers' retreat: Dove Cottage in Grasmere

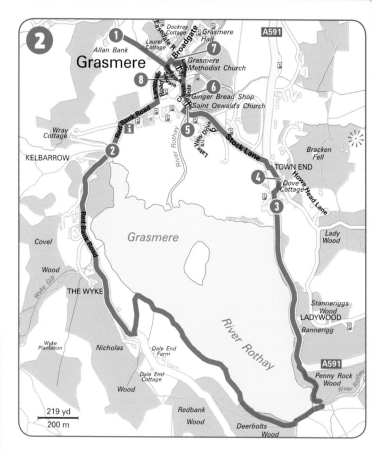

This circular tour takes you right into the Lake District and the pretty town of Grasmere. You'll visit two historically significant houses, go on a short walk and experience the region's export hit: gingerbread.

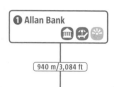

❶ Allan Bank

940 m / 3,084 ft

10:00am Your tour starts with a visit to ❶ Allan Bank → p. 44, the lovely villa that once belonged to Canon Rawnsley, founder of the National Trust. Can you feel yourself relaxing? The views of Lake Grasmere are impressive from the rooms, but even better from the sun loungers next to the building. Be sure to enjoy a stroll around the lake before bedtime.

At the centre of the village, turn right at _The Inn_ onto Langdale Road, then at the end right again on to Red

Bank. After about 1 km/0.6 mi on the left, you'll see a path beyond a wooden gate bearing the National Trust symbol – six oak leaves on a small branch. **Take the path down to ② Lake Grasmere** and delight in the views over this pretty, beautifully located lake.

Then cross the River Rothay, and after a while you'll come to the main road. Turn left to head back towards Grasmere, and on your left you'll see the ③ Daffodil Hotel *(Keswick Road | tel. 015394 6 35 50 | www.daff odilhotel.co.uk | Expensive)* – and it's time for lunch. From the restaurant you'll have INSIDER TIP fabulous views of the lake!

After lunch, **follow the road to the next stop: You'll soon be at ④ Dove Cottage → p. 44**, a former home of William Wordsworth. As you walk around the small, cosy rooms, you'll feel as if you have been transported back to the days of this important English poet.

Then continue **to Grasmere. When you have crossed the River Rothay, turn right onto the small cemetery of ⑤ St Oswald's Church. At the exit to the far end is the ⑥ Gingerbread Shop → p. 44.** Take a look around, and be sure to try the gingerbread, this delicious spicy biscuit.

`03:00pm` **Then have a walk around the town,** which also has the **⑦ Heaton Cooper Studio → p. 45** a delightful little art gallery with mainly landscapes. And you will certainly have earned your *cream tea* at **⑧ Baldry's Tea Room → p. 44** in the middle of Grasmere!

② Lake Grasmere 🌼 🏠	
3500 m/2.2 mi	
③ Daffodil Hotel 🍴 🌼	
130 m/427 ft	
④ Dove Cottage 🏛	
630 m/2,067 ft	
⑤ St. Oswald's Church ⛪	
70 m/229.7 ft	
⑥ Gingerbread Shop 🛍 🍴	
⑦ Heaton Cooper Studio 🏛 🛍	
140 m/459 ft	
⑧ Baldry's Tea Room ☕ 🍴	

Sweet treat: spicy gingerbread

③ BIKE RIDE AROUND WINDERMERE

START: ❶ Bowness-on-Windermere **END:** ❶ Bowness-on-Windermere	**7½ hours** Actual cycling time 2½ hours
Distance: easy 🚲 24 km/15 mi ▋▋ Height: 289 m/948 ft	

COSTS: approx. £60 per person for meals, admission charges, cycle hire and ferry

WHAT TO PACK: Rain jacket or sunscreen, depending on the weather, cycle helmet (available from the bike hire shop), bottle of water

IMPORTANT TIPS: Many hotels hire bikes, they are also available to hire from the Country Lanes Cycle Hire Centre *(tel. 015394 4 45 44 | www.countrylaneslakedistrict.co.uk)* at Windermere station.
Between Bowness and Wray Castle is route no. 6 of the National Cycle Network (blue signs with a white bike symbol and a white "6" against a red background).

On this circular tour, you'll cycle around the area to the west of Lake Windermere. You'll cross the lake by ferry and cycle along it, visit Wray Castle and places from the life of Beatrix Potter.

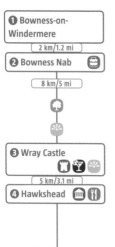

❶ Bowness-on-Windermere
　　2 km/1.2 mi
❷ Bowness Nab
　　8 km/5 mi
❸ Wray Castle
　　5 km/3.1 mi
❹ Hawkshead
　　5 km/3.1 mi

10:00am Start from ❶ Bowness-on-Windermere → p. 38 **and head south to the ferry terminal** ❷ **Bowness Nab.** The ferry will take you and your bike to the other side of Lake Windermere (ticket from the machine in the harbour, £1 each way). Once on the other side, **when you have left the ferry area head right along the narrow lakeside road.** Your destination is ❸ **Wray Castle** → p. 37 which is about 7 km/4.4 mi away. The route is hilly in places and has wonderful views of the lake. After a visit to Wray Castle, treat yourself to a cold drink, ideally outside somewhere so you can enjoy the fabulous views around you.

At lunchtime, continue the **5 km/3.1 mi to** ❹ **Hawkshead** → p. 36. There are lots of old farmhouses in this little town but its economy is based exclusively on the fame of the children's author Beatrix Potter. You can see her drawings at the **Beatrix Potter Gallery.** But now it's time for lunch! There are lots of pubs and cafés in Hawkshead, such as the **INSIDER TIP King's Arms** *(The Square | tel. 015394 3 63 72 | www.kingsarmshawkshead.co.uk | Moderate).* **Then leave Hawkshead on Main Street,**

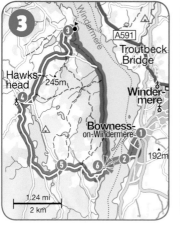

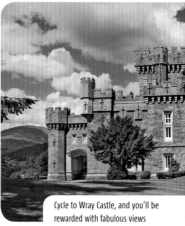

Cycle to Wray Castle, and you'll be rewarded with fabulous views

which is in the west. **Keep to the right of Esthwaite Water. After about 4 km/2.5 mi, cross Cunsey Beck and head right on the B5285.** Soon you'll see the entrance to ❺ **Hill Top → p. 36**, once the home of Beatrix Potter, which you can visit.

04:00pm **Continue along the road outside the house,** and you'll come to the ferry terminal. But shortly before you arrive there, **stop at** ❻ **Claife lookout point**, and enjoy the wonderful views of Windermere. At the café, enjoy a cream tea before heading **from the ferry terminal to the eastern shore of the lake and back to** ❶ **Bowness-on-Windermere**.

❺ Hill Top

3 km/1.9 mi

❻ Claife lookout point

3 km/1.9 mi

❶ Bowness-on-Windermere

➍ A WALK THROUGH KESWICK AND SURROUNDING AREA

START: ❶ Derwent Pencil Museum, Keswick
END: ❽ Royal Oak, Keswick

7 hours
Actual walking time
1½ hours

Distance:
🚶 approx. 5 km/3.1 mi

COSTS: approx. £35 per person for admission charges, boat, meals
WHAT TO PACK: Comfortable shoes, rain jacket or sunscreen depending on the weather, bottle of water

You'll see every side of the busy little town of Keswick on this short walk – including its quieter ones. You'll walk along Derwent Water, climb a small mountain and enjoy the views of this part of the Lake District.

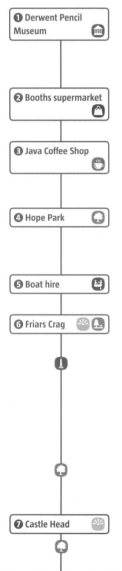

1 Derwent Pencil Museum 🏛

2 Booths supermarket 🛍

3 Java Coffee Shop ☕

4 Hope Park 🌳

5 Boat hire 🚣

6 Friars Crag 🌤🚤

❗

🌳

7 Castle Head 🌤

🌳

10:00am Begin your walk at the **1 Derwent Pencil Museum** → p. 67 on Carding Mill Lane. Find out here why the pencil is so closely linked to Keswick – graphite used to be mined in the area.

Leave the Pencil Museum heading for Main Street, and then stop at the big 2 Booths supermarket, where you can buy everything you need for a picnic. **Back on Main Street,** you'll come to the shopping area of Keswick. Stroll around the shops and treat yourself to a coffee, if you like, perhaps sitting outside at the **3 Java Coffee Shop** → p. 68.

Now turn right outside the coffee shop onto Lake Road, which will take you to Derwent Water → p. 68**. In 4 Hope Park**, a pretty green area, stop for a game of crazy golf. This will loosen you up before the upcoming boat trip.

Continue along the path, right past the Theatre by the Lake → p. 64, to the **5 boat hire** *(www.keswick-launch. co.uk),* where you can hire a rowing boat for an hour. **Then continue south along the shore to the lookout point 6 Friars Crag**. The perfect spot to enjoy the lunch you brought with you!

Then continue along the path (behind the bank and a memorial to the writer John Ruskin), heading away from the lake and towards a gate. **Cross two small bridges and follow the path to the left,** and you will come to a second gate. Here you'll **turn right, away from the lake and towards the main road. Cross the road carefully,** because there is the occasional car.

On the other side of the road, head through a gap and up a few steps, then follow the path into the wood. You'll come to a fairly wide path; turn right there, and keep going up the hill. At the top is a narrow path right to the top of 7 Castle Head. You've done it! Now, all you have to do is relax, and enjoy the fabulous views of Derwent Water. **Then go back down to the main route and**

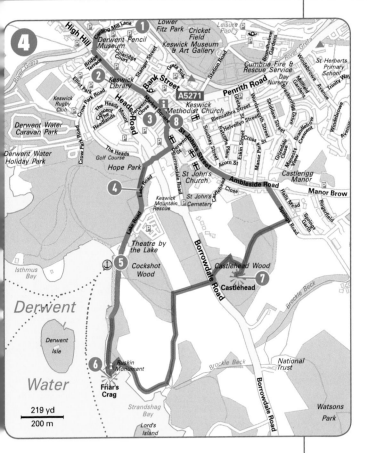

continue along the right, out of the wood and into a residential area. **At the end turn left onto Springs Road and stay on it until you reach the T-junction. Here, turn left onto Ambleside Road,** and continue along this until you are back in the town.

05:00pm At the end of this tour, reward yourself with a refreshing *pint* in a pub – ideally the ⑧ INSIDER TIP **Royal Oak** *(Main Street | tel. 017687 7 31 35 | Budget)* in the centre. Cheers!

⑧ Royal Oak

SPORTS & ACTIVITIES

Most people who come to the Lake District are looking for one thing: to be out and about in nature! For that reason, it is popular with tourists and locals alike. They want activity: to climb, cycle, get high up into the mountains, and above all to switch their mobiles off as quickly as possible. There are plenty of opportunities for people of every level of fitness to test their abilities.

CLIMBING

The Lake District is a popular area with climbers. Even beginners will find it relatively easy and safe to move along on a fixed-rope route, abseil down or try a rope garden, e.g. at *Keswick Extreme (Nichol End Marine | Portinscale |* Keswick | tel. 0800 0 0162 01 | www.kes wickextreme.com). The Honister Slate Mine (see p. 63) offers cave climbing and guided climbing tours in former mines.

CYCLING

Cyclists often have to use the roads in the Lake District because of a shortage of cycle paths. The National Cycle Network has details of partly traffic-free routes (blue signs with a bike symbol and a white number on a red square). Lots of hotels have bikes for guests to use and bigger towns have companies such as *E-Venture (from £20 per day | Elliot Park | Keswick | tel. 0778 3 82 27 22 | www. e-venturebikes.co.uk)* or *Country Lanes*

Walking, climbing, sailing, fishing – you simply have to be active in the Lake District. Or else relax in a spa!

(from £21 per day | Windermere station | tel. 015394 4 45 44 | www.countrylanes lakedistrict.co.uk).

FISHING

There is an abundance of trout, salmon and pike. Many fishing clubs offer day passes for non-members, including the *Esthwaite Trout Fishery (day pass £25 | The Boat House | Ridding Wood | Hawkshead | tel. 015394 3 65 41 | www. hawksheadtrout.com)* and the *Keswick Anglers Association (£7–25 depending on the type of fish | River Derwent | River Greta | www.keswickanglers.co.uk).* Fishing in Windermere, Ullswater and Coniston Water is free to everyone. However, you always require a permit from the Environment Agency, called a rod licence *(£6–12 per day depending on the type of fish | www.gov.uk/fish ing-licences).* They can be purchased from the local information centres of the National Park Authority (Bowness, Keswick, Ullswater).

HIKING

Without question the most popular type of activity in the Lake District! You can start almost anywhere and you will always find a lovely path to follow. Local book shops and tourist information centres stock plenty of maps. If you're looking for a challenge, try the Cumbria Way (www.cumbriaway.org): the 112 km/70 mi long route connects Ulverston and Carlisle in the Lake District. There are also numerous guided tours, the details of which are provided in leaflets in many hotels etc. The National Park Authority also offers occasional ● INSIDER TIP ▶ free guided walks *(www.lakedistrict.gov.uk/visiting/events)*.

GLIDING

Most gliding clubs also offer taster flights for beginners. After a few dry runs on the ground, you'll take off with one of the instructors for a short flight. Providers include *Eden Soaring (from £65 | Skelling Farm | Skirwith near Penrith | tel. 07849 97 95 75 | www.edensoaring. co.uk)* and the *Lakes Gliding Club (£80 | Walney Airfield | Barrow-in-Furness | tel. 07860 13 54 47 | www.lakesgc.co.uk)*.

OFF-ROADING & QUAD

Would you like to try your driving skills in the great outdoors? There are several routes for off-roaders and quads in the Lake District. Incidentally: if you don't want to drive yourself, you can also be a passenger. The providers include *Kankku (2 hours off-roader £175 per car | Victoria Forge | Victoria Street | Windermere | tel. 01539 44 74 14)* and *The Outdoor Activity Company (quad £50 per hour | Old Hutton near Kendal | tel. 01539 72 21 47 | www.theoutdooradven turecompany.co.uk)*.

PADDLING, SUP & RAFTING

● What good is the loveliest lake if all you do is stand on the shore? Canoes are kayaks are available to hire at all the major lakes in the Lake District. If you're not bothered about the level of comfort, why not try stand-up paddleboarding as well? Rafting is also possible at several places. One provider of canoes and kayaks is *Total Adventure (3 hours from £22 | 9 Church Street | Windermere | tel. 015394 4 3151)*. *Mobile Adventure (from £50 | 127 Main Street | Keswick | tel. 07960 87 55 63 | www.mobileadventure. co.uk)* arranges group tours.

PARAGLIDING

You need a little bit of courage, but as a beginner you can book a 30-minute tandem ride to help you get the hang (sorry) of it. Providers include *Extreme (tandem ride £120 | Braithwaite Farm | Braithwaite | tel. 017687 7 88 25 | www.jockysan derson.com)* or *Air Ventures (tandem ride £120 | The Orchard | Bassenthwaite | tel. 07830 28 19 86 | www.airventures.co.uk)*.

SAILING

Windermere, Ullswater and Derwent Water are the most popular lakes for sailing in the Lake District. However, the lakes are manageable in size and you usually end up back at the place where you hired the boat. They are available to hire e.g. from *Derwent Water Marina (from £30 per hour| Portinscale | Keswick | tel. 017687 7 29 12 | www.derwent watermarina.co.uk)*. You can hire boats from *Low Wood Bay Watersports Centre (Ambleside Road | Windermere | tel. 015394 3 94 41) (from £30 for 2 hours)* and complete a starter course *(£85 for 2 hours/1–2 people)*.

Upwards on Honister Pass: there are perfect walking trails all over the Lake District

TUBING

Something for those who have already done everything else you can do on water. You ride in a dinghy-like rubber ring down a white-water river (or something a little quieter for beginners). One organiser is *Keswick Extreme (from £25 for 2.5 hours| Nichol End Marine | Portinscale | Keswick | tel. 0800 0 0162 01 | www. keswickextreme.com).*

WATER SKIING & WAKEBOARDING

The classic among the action sports on water: water skiing and wakeboarding are also available in some parts of the Lake District. The best-known provider is the *Low Wood Bay Watersports Centre (£55 for 30 minutes | Ambleside Road | Windermere | tel. 015394 3 94 41 | www.englishlakes.co.uk/low-wood-bay)* on Windermere.

WELLNESS

What's better than a hotel with a spa? Try the *Beech Hill Hotel (Newby Bridge Road | Windermere | tel. 0844 5 02 75 87 (*) | beechhillhotel.co.uk/ spa)* or the *Swan Hotel (Newby Bridge | tel. 015395 3 16 81 | www.swanhotel. com)*, both on Windermere. These spa areas can sometimes be used by non-residents for a fee.

WINDSURFING

Even though Cumbria doesn't necessarily instantly spring to mind as a surfing hotspot, the Lake District is ideal, especially for beginners. Windermere and Derwent Water both suitable for familiarising yourself with windsurfing. There are beginners' courses at *Derwent Water Marina (half day £77 | www.derwentwatermarina.co.uk).*

TRAVEL WITH KIDS

Forget about the big leisure parks and multiplex cinemas – the kid's programme in the Lake District is a little more down-to-earth (literally).

You might find your little ones take a little persuading before you can convince them to walk up a mountain with you. But as with most children, once they get to the top, they just want more. Many sights are aimed at children. With the *Treasure Trails (www. treasuretrails.co.uk/things-to-do/cum bria)*, children can set off on a treasure hunt in several places throughout the Lake District. The tours are available as a PDF file online. It is usually cheaper to book tickets online in advance, and there are almost always discounts for families. Ps – the storybook character Peter Rabbit is the star of the National Park. He's available as a stuffed toy everywhere and around Windermere in particular.

WINDERMERE & THE SOUTH EAST

THE COCOA BEAN COMPANY
(126 B2) (*M E6–7*)

At this shop in Hawkshead, children and teenagers between the ages of two and 18 learn how to make their own chocolate. There are workshops all day, and only groups need to book in advance. *March–Oct daily from 9am–6pm, Nov–Feb from 10am–4pm | workshop £16 | Main Street | Hawkshead | www.the cocoabeancompany.com/hawkshead*

Fun and games: children can balance on a Skywalk, take alpacas for a walk and make their own chocolate in the Lake District

GO APE! (126 B3) (*⌖ E7*)

A huge adventure playground in the forest: on the Skywalk, you can swing through the forest high above the ground, cross rope bridges and fly on (well secured) zip wires as if on a jungle camp. You can also hire Segways to explore other parts of Grizedale. Go Ape! also operates another, smaller park in Whinlatter near Keswick. *Feb–Nov daily from 9am–4pm | admission £33, children £25 (admission from age 10 years) | Grizedale | Hawkshead | www.goape.co.uk*

LAKELAND MINIATURE VILLAGE (125 F5) (*⌖ E9*)

The Lakeland Miniature Village contains minature slate versions of more than 100 buildings in the National Park, including Beatrix Potter's Hill Top and the Bridge House at Ambleside. You'll feel like a giant on Lilliput as you walk around them. *March–Oct daily from 10.30am–5pm | admission £4, children £2 | Coach House Winder Lane | Flookburgh | Grange-over-Sands | www.lakelandminiaturevillage.co.uk*

STOTT PARK BOBBIN MILL
(126 B3) (*ಐ E7*)

In the 19th century, some 250 men and boys worked in this former bobbin mill – and you can go back to those days. Dress your children up in clothes of the era (basic costumes are available) and explore the old buildings – there are still a lot of machines to see. Regular displays. *April–Aug daily, Sept/Oct Wed–Sun 10am–5pm | admission £7.60, children £4.60 | Finsthwaite | Ulverston | www.english-heritage.org.uk*

CONISTON & THE SOUTH WEST

CONISTON BOATING CENTRE
(126 A2) (*ಐ E7*)

Get out on the water – you can easily take the whole family out in a canoe or kayak on Coniston Water. Boats are available by the hour, and life jackets for emergencies are included. *Daily from 10am–5pm | From £15 per hour depending on boat | Lake Road | Coniston | www.conistonboatingcentre.co.uk*

CUSTOM HOUSE
(125 D5–6) (*ಐ C–D9*)

The former customs house at Barrow-in-Furness has been turned into an entertainment centre. The attractions include Play Zone, a whole floor for children under 8 years of age. Older children can chase each other around a different floor at laser tag. *Daily 9.30am–5.15pm | admission £4 | 1 Abbey Road | Barrow-in-Furness | www.1abbeyroad.co.uk/playzone*

DERWENT WATER & THE NORTH WEST

ALPACALY EVER AFTER
(121 D5) (*ಐ D4*)

Have you ever INSIDER TIP taken an alpaca for a walk? This cute little type of camel lives in various part of the Lake District, where it feels completely at home in the climate. On the Lingholm Estate on Derwent Water you can take the (usually) calm, very sociable animals for a walk. A great way to spend some time! *Daily 9am–5.30pm | from £60 for 1.5 hours | Lingholm Estate | Portinscale | Keswick | tel. 017687 7 42 38 | www.alpacalyeverafter.co.uk*

KESWICK CLIMBING WALL
(121 E5) (*ಐ D4*)

A whole park to wear yourselves out in: you can transition smoothly from the giant climbing wall to canoeing, hang over a river well-secured to a rope, or zip through the landscape. Once back on the ground, try your hand with a bow and arrow. *Daily 9am–6pm | admission from £7 (children and adults) | Goosewell Farm | Keswick | www.keswickclimbingwall.co.uk*

LAKE DISTRICT COAST AQUARIUM
(120 B4) (*ಐ B3*)

Admittedly, there are no vast glass containers that you can walk beneath and watch brightly-coloured fish from all over the world in this aquarium. But it's a great opportunity to experience close up what most people don't get to see on a visit to the Lake District: its river and maritime world. 150 types of fish, all from the region, live in the 35 tanks of the aquarium. *Daily 10am–5pm | admission £8.50, children £5.50 | South Quay | Maryport | www.coastaquarium.co.uk*

WEST COAST INDOOR KARTING
(120 B4) (*ಐ B3*)

When your children have had enough of the mountains and lakes, you can let them get behind the steering wheel here. The only condition: they must be at least eight years old. The whole

How about a walk? Why not rent an alpaca!

route is housed in a former industrial warehouse, so it can be used whatever the weather. *Tue–Fri 1pm–10pm, Sat/Sun 10am–10pm | From £20, children from £15 | Solway Trading Estate | Maryport | www.westcoastkarting.co.uk*

ULLSWATER & THE NORTH EAST

CRAFTY MONKEYS STUDIO
(122–123 C–D 4–5) (*⌖ F4*)

The visitors are the artists here. At this studio in Penrith, children can throw pots or figures in clay and create pictures from tiny pieces of mosaic. Pottery items will be fired and can be collected later. *Wed–Sat 10am–3pm, Sun 11am–4pm | From £9 to throw an item | 3 Corney Square | Penrith | www.craftymonkeys.org*

PENRITH LEISURE CENTRE ●
(122–123 C–D 4–5) (*⌖ F4*)

This swimming pool helps on rainy days. A number of diving platforms, a 25 m/

82 ft pool, fitness equipment, badminton courts and a bowling alley will help you forget even the heaviest downpour. *Mon–Fri 6.30am–10pm, Sat 7.30am–8pm, Sun 7.30am–9pm | admission £6.30, children £4.50 | Southend Road | Penrith | short.travel/lkd10*

RHEGED (122 C5) (*⌖ F4*)

Crawl inside this fortress, and play as if your life depends on it: Rheged is like a medieval building inside a hill. Inside are play corners for children, a 3D cinema showing children's films, a children's theatre, and somewhere to paint ceramics. And while the youngsters are busy doing all that, their parents can relax in the spa or visit one of the many restaurants. *Daily 10am–5.30pm | admission free, although there is a charge for some activities | Redhills | Penrith | www.rheged.com*

FESTIVALS & EVENTS

FEBRUARY

Keswick Film Festival (www.keswickfilm club.org): small festival with a focus on short films (from mid-Feb).

MARCH

Penrith goes Orange (short.travel/lkd1): The marmalade festival in Dalemain has become an orange festival. Always the middle of March.

APRIL

Damson Day Country Fair (www.damson day.co.uk): This farmers' festival at the end of April near Crosthwaite is all about damsons, but there's also music, food and lots of beer.

MAY

Keswick Jazz and Blues Festival (www. keswickjazzandbluesfestival.co.uk): In mid-May this little town spends four days celebrating jazz and blues concerts.

JUNE

Country Fest Crooklands (www.westmor landshow.co.uk/country-fest): Country show near Kendal at the beginning of June, a combination of animal shows, crafts, food and farming.

Keswick Mountain Festival (www.keswick mountainfestival.co.uk): Major outdoor event on Derwent Water in Keswick. It's not just about walking and climbing – there's live music in the evenings too (mid-June).

JULY

Derwent Water Regatta (short.travel/ lkd2): A still relatively new regatta that takes place in mid-July with mainly small boats taking over Derwent Water at Crow Park in Keswick.

Rock the Fells (www.rockthefells.com): This one-day rock festival in Bootle at the end of July features mostly unknown British artists – but the music is very good.

INSIDER TIP ▶ *Kendal Calling Festival*: (www. kendalcalling.co.uk): Four days of open-air festival at Lowther Deer Park, always at the end of July and with high-calibre rock and pop bands.

AUGUST

Cartmel Show (www.cartmelagricultural society.org.uk): Agricultural show and festival at the beginning of August in Cartmel with plenty of food.

Lowther Show (www.lowthershow.co.uk): Fishing, riding competitions and plenty

of food are offered on the castle site of Lowther in mid-August.

Grasmere Sports and Show *(www.grasmeresports.com)*: A combination of sports day and a summer show. The main attractions at this event at the end of August are races and wrestling.

SEPTEMBER

Chilli Fest *(www.holker.co.uk)*: There's plenty to eat at this food festival at Holker Hall early in September – most of it including chilli.

Lakes Alive *(www.lakesalive.co.uk)*: Art and culture festival in and around Kendal, always in mid-September.

Taste Cockermouth *(short.travel/lkd11)*: On the last weekend in September, Cockermouth becomes a gourmet town with lots of food stands.

OCTOBER

Wasdale Head Show & Shepherd's Meet *(www.wasdaleheadshow.co.uk)*: Farm show in mid-October with lots of sporting activities and competitions.

NOVEMBER

INSIDER TIP ▶ Holker Winter Market: *(short.travel/lkd3)*: An early Christmas market on Holker Estate near Cartmel – there's an excellent selection of crafts on sale at this annual event.

DECEMBER

Christmas markets: The German custom has spread to the Lake District. Towns like Cockermouth, Windermere and Ulverston now hold their own Christmas markets in December, but usually only over one weekend.

PUBLIC HOLIDAYS

1 Jan	New Year's Day
19 April 2019, 10 April 2020, 2 April 2021	Good Friday
22 April 2019, 13 April 2020, 5 April 2021	Easter Monday
23 April	St. George's Day (national holiday)
First Monday in May	May Day Holiday
Last Monday in May	Spring Bank Holiday
Last Monday in August	Summer Bank Holiday
25 Dec	Christmas Day
26 Dec	Boxing Day

LINKS, BLOGS, APPS & MORE

www.lakeswalks.co.uk For keen walkers: This website contains a wide range of walks in the Lake District with precise details of the routes, some with photos and videos of the main points

blog.golakes.co.uk First-hand information: The Lake District's official blog with lots of idea and suggestions for special occasions – walks, celebrations and more

englishlakes.wordpress.com Life in the Lake District: This private blog is dedicated to life in the National Park with lots of tips on walks and lovely photos

www.englishlakes.blog Tourism blog, mainly with news of the latest developments concerning various attractions, hotels and gastronomy. Regular tips for excursions in and around the Lake District

www.lakedistrict.gov.uk/the-blog The official blog of the Lake District National Park Authority deals mainly with people and possibilities in the region. You'll learn a lot about current offers, food and the sights

www.thewestmorlandgazette.co.uk This weekly newspaper from the southern Lake District reports on current events in the region, plus traffic developments and new openings etc.

whc.unesco.org/en/list/422 The Lake District has been a Unesco World Heritage Site since 2017. The organisation explains on its website why this is so, and provides documents and plenty of lovely photos

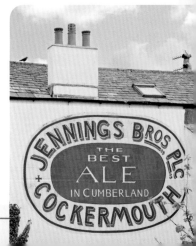

www.visitcumbria.com/webcams Have a look at the Lake District: you'll find several webcams here. Really useful in the morning for checking out the weather in the various parts of the National Park

Regardless of whether you are still researching your trip or are already in the Lake District: these addresses will provide you with more information, videos and networks to make your holiday even more enjoyable

VIDEOS & MUSIC

short.travel/lkd4 Time lapse of a whole year in the Lake District: this short BBC video consists of elaborate scenes of the National Park, some filmed by drones

short.travel/lkd5 The Lake District even looks fabulous in black and white: videos of bygone times, mainly the 1930s and 40s

short.travel/lkd6 We are absolutely convinced you will book your holiday as soon as you have seen this video. On this short trip through the Lake District, the National Park was filmed mainly from above

APPS

Stagecoach Bus This app provided by the coach operator, Stagecoach, has routes and a timetable. Really useful if you're travelling around the Lake District on public transport (for iOS, Android)

The Trainline Essential for rail travel in Great Britain. The Trainline always seeks the best-value connections, and you can buy your ticket online straight away (for iOS, Android)

Days Out Preservation on your smartphone – English Heritage tells you which of the organisation's properties are in your area (for iOS, Android, Windows)

National Trust This App not only tells you which National Trust properties are in your area, but you can also search the whole of Great Britain for estates, castles and land (for iOS, Android, Windows)

Met Office What's the forecast for today? This app by the government's met office will tell you. Detailed and regional maps (for iOS, Android)

TRAVEL TIPS

ACCOMMODATION

BED & BREAKFAST (B&B)

B&Bs used to be a cheaper option, but these days they're roughly the same price as hotels. Expect to pay about £40 per person.

HOLIDAY APARTMENTS

Major providers are Holiday Lettings *(www.holidaylettings.co.uk)*, Hoseasons *(www.hoseasons.co.uk)* and, of course, Airbnb *(www.airbnb.co.uk)*. The National Trust *(tel. 0344 800 2070 (*) | www.nationaltrust.org.uk/holidays)* also rents out INSIDER TIP rooms and holiday apartments on its properties as well as entire cottages.

HOTELS

There is a wide selection of hotels in the Lake District: boutique, spa to country house hotels. The major chains haven't really established themselves in the region. This lack of competition means prices can be quite high.

YOUTH HOSTELS

Youth hostels have overcome their poor dormitory reputation, and now often offer private rooms as well, although don't expect a very high level of comfort. The official association is the *Youth Hostel Association (YHA | Trevelyan House | Dimple Road | Matlock | tel. 01629 59 2700 | www.yha.org.uk)*, and it has a number of hostels in fabulous countryside locations.

ADMISSION CHARGES

Admission charges in the Lake District can be higher than comparable attractions in other countries. Once a year, always at the beginning of September, you can take advantage of the ● *Heritage Open Days (www. heritageopendays. org.uk)* and visit lots of excellent sights free of charge, including lots of private buildings that are otherwise closed to the public.

ARRIVAL

🚗 If you come from abroad by car, the Eurotunnel is the quickest way to cross the English Channel. However, you'll then have a drive of about six hours ahead of you before you get to the Lake District. Depending on the time of day, there is a train every 20 to 40 minutes between Calais in France and Folkestone in England. Single ticket per vehicle and journey from £62. *www. eurotunnel.com*

RESPONSIBLE TRAVEL

It doesn't take a lot to be environmentally friendly whilst travelling. Don't just think about your carbon footprint whilst flying to and from your holiday destination but also about how you can protect nature and culture abroad. As a tourist it is especially important to respect nature, look out for local products, cycle instead of driving, save water and much more. If you would like to find out more about eco-tourism please visit: *www.ecotourism.org*

From arrival to weather

Your holiday from start to finish: the most important addresses and information for your trip to the Lake District

The Eurostar high-speed train also travels through the Eurotunnel, linking Paris and Brussels with St Pancras station in London (travel time about 2 hours). From Euston Station (not far from the Eurostar stop at St Pancras) it's about another 4 hours to the Lake District.

Overnight ferries are one practical solution for the north of England. DFDS *(www.dfdsseaways.com)* has one crossing a day from IJmuiden near Amsterdam to Newcastle *(crossing time 16.5 hours, from £155/$192 per route with car and cabin)*. From there it's about an hour and a half to the Lake District. P&O *(www.poferries.com, from £155/$192 per route)* has two crossings a day from Rotterdam and Zeebrügge to Hull. From there it's about 2.5 hours to the Lake District. As a general rule, be sure to book in advance because it's cheaper, and the ferries are often fully booked at peak season. The ADAC offers its members often significant discounts on these routes.

From Dover it's about 6 hours by car to the Lake District. There are crossings to Dover from Calais (1.5 hours) and Dunkirk (2 hours) (DFDS, P&O, from about £45/$55 per route including car and passengers). There are other ferry connections: Hoek–Harwich (6.5–9.5 hours, *www.stenaline.co.uk*), Newhaven–Dieppe (4 hours, DFDS), Roscoff–Plymouth (5.5 hours), Cherbourg–Poole (4.5 hours), St Malo/Cherbourg/Caen–Portsmouth (3–11 hours, *www.brittany ferries.co.uk*).

Practical airports for a visit to the Lake District are Newcastle, Leeds, Manchester and Liverpool, some of which are served directly from several British airports (e.g. with British Airways). Carlisle airport has plans for passenger flights starting spring 2019 to destinations in the UK and Ireland. For US visitors, Thomas Cook offers a nonstop flight from JFK to Manchester for example.

BUDGETING

Cream tea	£5.30/ $7.40
	for a cream tea
Beer	£4.00/$5.50
	for a pint (0.568 l) in a pub
Souvenir	£12/$16
	for a mug with a sheep motif (Herdy)
Petrol	£1.20/$1.60
	for 1 l petrol/diesel
Boat hire	£13.40/$18.50
	for one hour
Parking	£1/$1.40
	per hour in a multi-storey car park

CAMPING

Wild camping is not usually allowed in England, but is tolerated within reasonable limits as long as you tidy up afterwards. There are official sites everywhere. Information is available from the tourist centres and from the Camping & Caravanning Club *(www.campingand caravanningclub.co.uk)*.

CONSULATES AND EMBASSIES

EMBASSY OF IRELAND
17 Grosvenor Place | Belgravia | London | www.dfa.ie/irish-embassy/great-britain | tel. 020 7235 2171

HIGH COMMISSION OF AUSTRALIA
Strand | London | www.uk.embassy.gov.au | tel. 020 7379 4334

HIGH COMMISSION OF CANADA
Canada House | Trafalgar Square | London | www.canadainternational.gc.ca/united_kingdom-royaume_uni/index.aspx?lang=eng | tel. 020 7004 6000

U.S. EMBASSY
24 Grosvenor Square | London | uk.usembassy.gov | tel. 020 7499 9000

CUSTOMS

UK citizens do not have to pay any duty on goods brought from another EU country as long as tax was included in the price and the items are for private consumption only. Tax free allowances include: 800 cigarettes, 400 small cigars, 200 cigars, 1kg/2.2lbs pipe tobacco, 10L spirits, 20L liqueurs, 90L wine, 110L beer. Those travelling from the USA, Canada, Australia or other non-EU countries are allowed to enter with the following tax-free amounts: 200 cigarettes or 100 small cigars or 50 cigars or 250g pipe tobacco. 2L wine and spirits with less than 22 vol. % alcohol, 1L spirits with more than 22 vol. % alcohol content.

American passport holders returning to the USA do not have to pay duty on articles purchased overseas up to the value of $800, but there are limits on the amount of alcoholic beverages and tobacco products. For regulations for international travel for U.S. residents see *www.cbp.gov*.

DRIVING

The Lake District is full of single track roads, often with lots of tight bends which can be difficult to navigate. The main thing for people who come from abroad is: drive on the left and don't forget that you have to overtake on the right!
Some other driving tips for foreign visitors: There are relatively few traffic signs, but lots of traffic lights, giveway signs and even more roundabouts.

FOR FILM BUFFS

Miss Potter – (2006) Chris Noonan's sensitive film drama is a fairy-tale rendering of the life of writer Beatrix Potter. Much of the film was actually shot in the Lake District, where Potter lived. With Renée Zellweger and Ewan McGregor

Peter Rabbit – (2018) The latest treat for fans of Miss Potter: Peter Rabbit, her storybook bunny, comes to life in this part-animated 3D film for children. The story is basically about how Peter keeps eating Mr. McGregor's crops, which drives him crazy. Director Will Gluck had parts of the film shot in the Lake District, which is also where the story takes place. With Rose Byrne, Domhnall Gleeson and Sam Neill

Traffic already on a roundabout has priority. The maximum speed in built-up areas is usually 48 km/h/30 mph, otherwise on ordinary roads 96 km/h/60 mph, and on dual carriageways with a barrier between carriageways and motorways it's 112 km/h/70 mph.

People caught speeding or otherwise violating the traffic laws can expect a large fine. The alcohol limit is 0.8, but be aware of the risks of driving under the influence of alcohol. Seatbelts are compulsory, and speaking on a mobile phone while driving is illegal.

ELECTRICITY

The mains voltage is 240 volts. Plugs are different from the ones in Central Europe, and you will require a three-pole adapter (type G).

EMERGENCY SERVICES

– tel. 999 and 112
– The Lake District Search and Mountain Rescue Association provides tips on its website to help prevent emergencies: www.ldsamra.org.uk.

HEALTH

In Great Britain, the state National Health Service (NHS) guarantees free healthcare for everyone, although EU citizens still have to present a European Health Insurance Card (EHIC). Foreign health insurance is a good idea to cover more complicated accidents or even transportation home. Pharmacies can be found in all major supermarkets and at the nationwide chain Boots.

IMMIGRATION

Citizens of the UK & Ireland, USA, Canada, Australia and New Zealand need only a valid passport to enter all countries of the EU. Children below the age of 12 need a children's passport. Check online for the latest travel advice and entry requirements: www.gov.uk/foreign-travel-advice (UK Citizens) or www.state.gov/travel (US Citizens)

INFORMATION

The internet provides much helpful information for visitors of the United Kingdom in general as well as the Lake District in particular. Two informative websites are:
www.visitbritain.com/gb
www.golakes.co.uk

INTERNET CAFES & WIFI

Almost every hotel and restaurant, pub and even major supermarket offers free wifi. Now that roaming charges have been abolished within the EU, Europeans can use their usual data in England without having to pay extra. But it's always advisable to check with your provider first!

MEDIA

The BBC (British Broadcasting Corporation) has countless TV and radio channels and stations. Pay-as-you-go Sky is widely available, and free in many hotels. The daily newspapers are mainly national publications that tend to be more political than in other countries. The more serious newspapers are The Guardian (liberal democratic), The Times, Daily Telegraph (both conservative) and the business newspaper The Financial Times. One local radio station is Lakeland Radio, and the BBC broadcasts to almost every part of the Lake District.

MONEY & CREDIT CARDS

The currency is the British Pound or sterling. There are 100 pence in one pound. Credit cards are widely accepted even for very small amounts. Bank are usually open Mon–Fri from 10am until 5pm, and even very small towns and villages will have a cash machine (ATM), often in a food shop or post office or at a petrol station. If you are asked whether you want to pay in pounds or euros, always select pounds at the machine because this usually gives you a much better exchange rate! There are a few exchange bureaus, and if you go to one in a branch of Marks & Spencer you will not be charged an exchange fee.

OPENING HOURS

The main opening times are Mon–Sat 10am–5.30pm, although some shops open before then and stay open for longer, especially the supermarkets in bigger towns. You can also shop on Sundays in many places in the Lake District (usually from noon until 5pm). Many of the smaller shops are also open on bank holidays.

PHONE & MOBILE PHONE

Better not to plan any telephone conferences in the Lake District! Reception in towns is usually good, but sooner or later you will come to a dead spot in the mountains.

The main mobile phone companies are Vodafone, EE, Three and O2. All providers also have prepaid cards. Reasonable networks for them are Virgin, Tesco, Sainsbury's and Three. The dialling code for Great Britain is 0044. When calling from abroad, omit the '0' of the area code or the first zero on mobile num-

WEATHER IN AMBLESIDE

	Jan	Feb	March	April	May	June	July	Aug	Sept	Oct	Nov	Dec
Daytime temperature in °C/°F	7/45	7/45	9/48	12/54	16/61	18/64	20/68	20/68	17/63	13/55	10/50	7/45
Night-time temperatures in °C/°F	1/34	1/34	3/37	4/40	7/45	10/50	12/54	11/52	9/48	7/45	4/39	2/36
Sunshine hours/day	2	2	3	4	5	5	5	4	3	2	2	1
Precipitation days/month	19	15	16	13	12	12	13	15	14	19	18	16

bers. The UK dialling code for the USA and Canada is 001, for Australia 0061, and for Ireland 00353. Omit any leading '1' in North American numbers and any first zero in Australian or Irish numbers. Operator: within the UK 100, international 155.

POST

Post offices in the countryside and in towns are increasingly part of stationery shops, petrol stations and supermarkets, and accordingly may well be open for longer. Official post offices are open Mon–Fri 9am–5.30pm and Sat 9am–12.30pm. It will cost you £1.17 to send a letter or postcard to another European country.

PUBLIC TRANSPORT

Stagecoach (www.stagecoachbus.com) operates a network of coaches on the main roads of the Lake District, although the timetable is a little thin. If you are planning to travel by public transport, be sure to organise it well. The brochure The Lakes Connection (free of charge from railway stations, tourist information centres and many supermarkets) has the bus timetables and lots of discount vouchers for attractions in the National Park.

The Central Lakes Day Rider Pass costs £5.50 and offers a day's unlimited bus travel in the central Lake District. The Lakes Day Ranger Ticket (£20.50) provides a day's travel on most of the train routes in the National Park. Carlisle, Penrith, Windermere as well as Oxenholme near Kendal have direct connections to towns in Scotland and other parts of England. There are also local railways to Windermere and along the coast.

TAXI

It's a good idea to book one by phone (numbers will differ depending on your location), although bigger towns like Cockermouth, Keswick and Kendal will usually have a taxi rank in the centre.

TIME

The time is Greenwich Mean Time (GMT).

TIPPING

The usual amount to tip in restaurants is about 10 percent of the total bill (depending on how satisfied you are) – unless the bill gives a service charge at the bottom. You don't normally tip at the bar in pubs. As elsewhere in the world, hotel staff and taxi drivers will usually appreciate a little token.

Idyllic Caldbeck

ROAD ATLAS

Photo: Dry-stone wall on Black Crag near Coniston

Exploring the Lake District

The map on the back cover shows how the area has been sub-divided

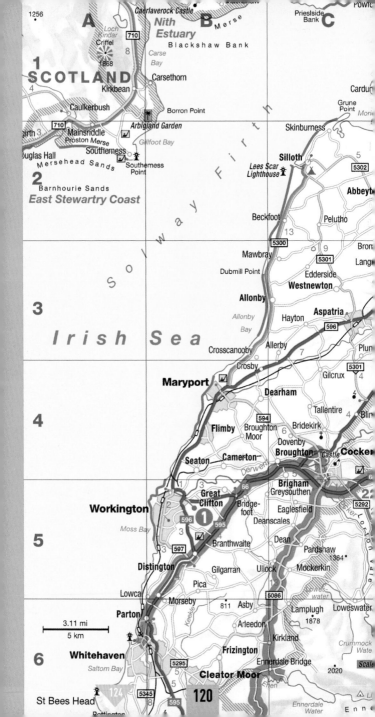

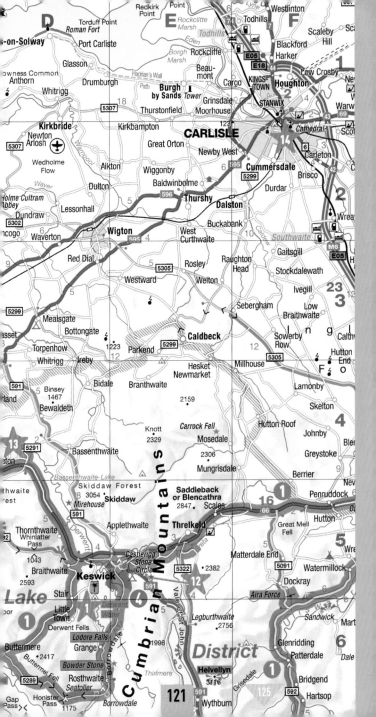

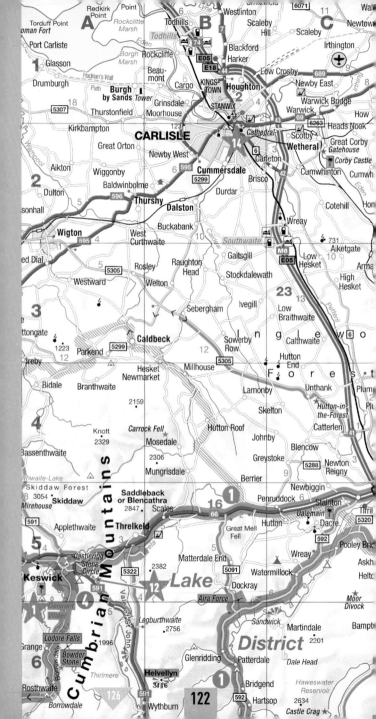

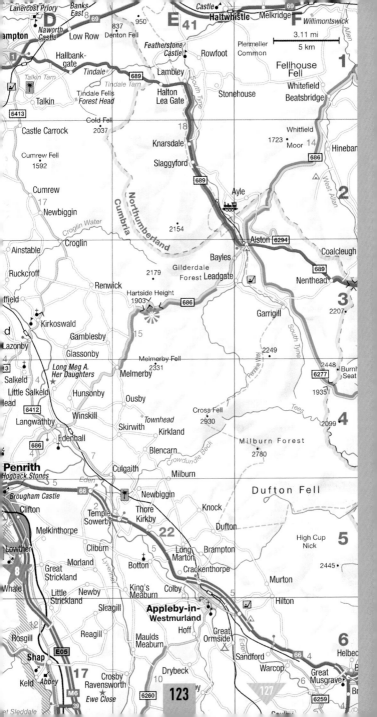

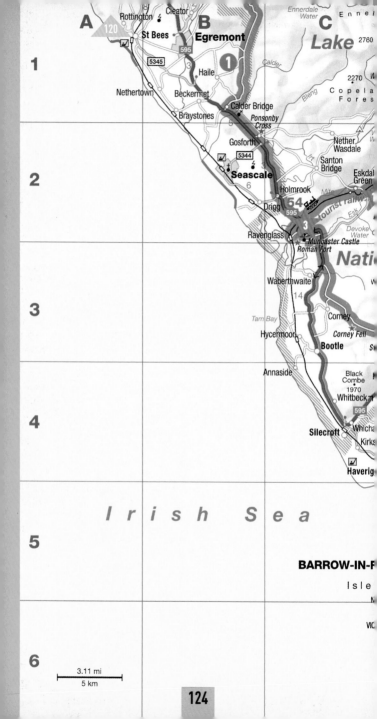

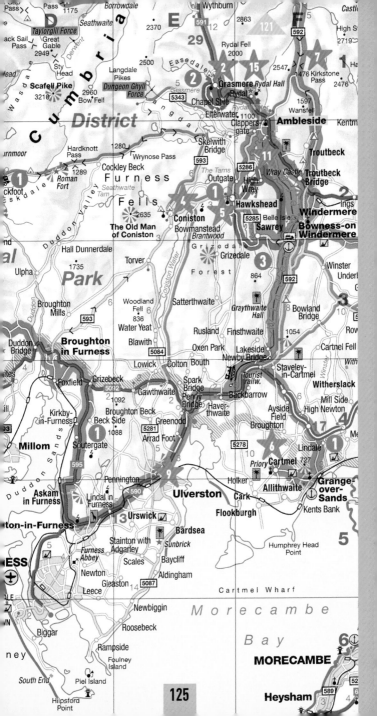

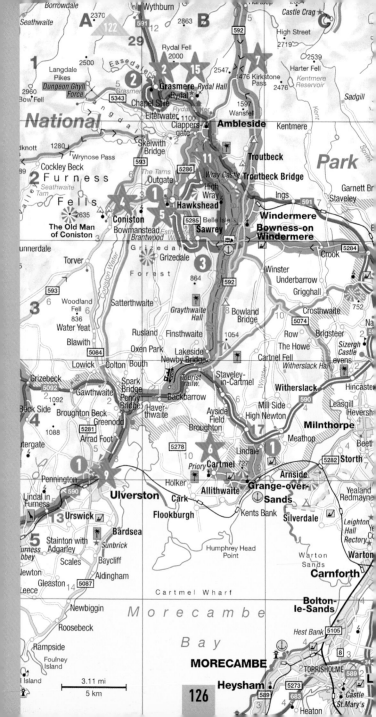

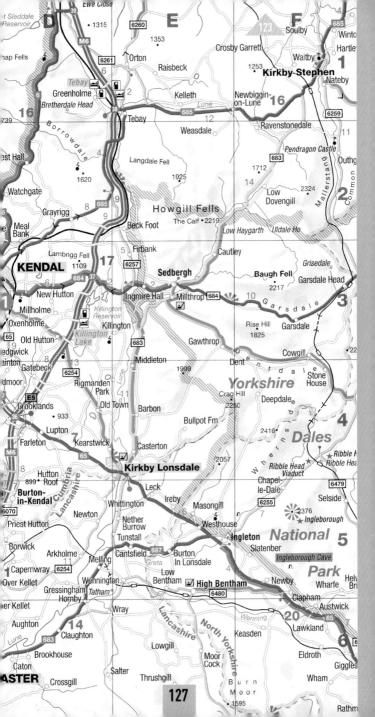

KEY TO ROAD ATLAS

Autobahn mit Anschlussstelle und Anschlussnummern	Viernheim (45)-(6)-(45)-(36)-(24)-(12)	Motorway with junction and junction number
Autobahn in Bau mit voraussichtlichem Fertigstellungsdatum	Datum ├ ─ ─ ─ ┤ Date	Motorway under construction with expected date of opening
Rasthaus mit Übernachtung · Raststätte	🛏 Kassel ✕	Hotel, motel · Restaurant
Kiosk · Tankstelle	▭ 🅿	Snackbar · Filling-station
Autohof · Parkplatz mit WC	🚚 P	Truckstop · Parking place with WC
Autobahn-Gebührenstelle	▬▬▬■▬▬▬	Toll station
Autobahnähnliche Schnellstraße	════════	Dual carriageway with motorway characteristics
Fernverkehrsstraße	▬▬▬▬▬▬	Trunk road
Verbindungsstraße	▬▬▬▬▬▬	Main road
Nebenstraßen	▬▬▬ ▬▬	Secondary roads
Fahrweg · Fußweg	··········	Carriageway · Footpath
Gebührenpflichtige Straße	┼┼┼┼┼┼┼	Toll road
Straße für Kraftfahrzeuge gesperrt	─X─X─X─X─	Road closed for motor vehicles
Straße für Wohnanhänger gesperrt	🚫▶ ◀🚫	Road closed for caravans
Straße für Wohnanhänger nicht empfehlenswert	🚫▶ ◀🚫	Road not recommended for caravans
Autofähre · Autozug-Terminal	─🚢─ ─🚂	Car ferry · Autorail station
Hauptbahn · Bahnhof · Tunnel	▬▬o▬▬)▬(▬	Main line railway · Station · Tunnel
Besonders sehenswertes kulturelles Objekt	Neuschwanstein	Cultural site of particular interest
Besonders sehenswertes landschaftliches Objekt	Breitachklamm	Landscape of particular interest
MARCO POLO Erlebnistour 1	▬▬▬▬▬▬	MARCO POLO Discovery Tour 1
MARCO POLO Erlebnistouren	▬▬▬▬▬▬	MARCO POLO Discovery Tours
MARCO POLO Highlight	☆	MARCO POLO Highlight
Landschaftlich schöne Strecke	▬▬▬▬▬▬	Route with beautiful scenery
Touristenstraße	Hanse-Route	Tourist route
Museumseisenbahn	🚂▬▬▬🚃	Tourist train
Kirche, Kapelle · Kirchenruine Kloster · Klosterruine	✝ ⚲ ✝ ✲	Church, chapel · Church ruin Monastery · Monastery ruin
Schloss, Burg · Burgruine Turm · Funk-, Fernsehturm	♜ ♟ 🏛 ♖	Palace, castle · Castle ruin Tower · Radio or TV tower
Leuchtturm · Windmühle Denkmal · Soldatenfriedhof	⚲ ✗ ⚱ ⌂	Lighthouse · Windmill Monument · Military cemetery
Ruine, frühgeschichtliche Stätte · Höhle Hotel, Gasthaus, Berghütte · Heilbad	∴ ⋒ 🏠 ♨	Archaeological excavation, ruins · Cave Hotel, inn, refuge · Spa
Campingplatz · Jugendherberge Schwimmbad, Erlebnisbad, Strandbad · Golfplatz	△ △ △ ⌐ ⚑	Camping site · Youth hostel Swimming pool, leisure pool, beach · Golf-course
Botanischer Garten, sehenswerter Park · Zoologischer Garten	🌳 🦒	Botanical gardens, interesting park · Zoological garden
Bedeutendes Bauwerk · Bedeutendes Areal	▪ ★	Important building · Important area
Verkehrsflughafen · Regionalflughafen	✈ ⊕	Airport · Regional airport
Flugplatz · Segelflugplatz	⊕ ⌖	Airfield · Gliding site
Boots- und Jachthafen	⚓	Marina

Höhenangaben in Fuß Entfernungen in Meilen	Altitude in feet Distances in miles

MARCO POLO TRAVEL GUIDES

Algarve
Amsterdam
Andalucia
Athens
Australia
Austria
Bali & Lombok
Bangkok
Barcelona
Berlin
Brazil
Bruges
Brussels
Budapest
Bulgaria
California
Cambodia
Canada East
Canada West / Rockies & Vancouver
Cape Town & Garden Route
Cape Verde
Channel Islands
Chicago & The Lakes
China
Cologne
Copenhagen
Corfu
Costa Blanca & Valencia
Costa Brava
Costa del Sol & Granada
Crete
Cuba
Cyprus (North and South)
Devon & Cornwall
Dresden
Dubai
Dublin

Dubrovnik & Dalmatian Coast
Edinburgh
Egypt
Egypt Red Sea Resorts
Finland
Florence
Florida
French Atlantic Coast
French Riviera (Nice, Cannes & Monaco)
Fuerteventura
Gran Canaria
Greece
Hamburg
Hong Kong & Macau
Ibiza
Iceland
India
India South
Ireland
Israel
Istanbul
Italy
Japan
Jordan
Kos
Krakow
Lake District
Lake Garda
Lanzarote
Las Vegas
Lisbon
London
Los Angeles
Madeira & Porto Santo
Madrid
Mallorca
Malta & Gozo
Mauritius
Menorca

Milan
Montenegro
Morocco
Munich
Naples & Amalfi Coast
New York
New Zealand
Norway
Oslo
Oxford
Paris
Peru & Bolivia
Phuket
Portugal
Prague
Rhodes
Rome
Salzburg
San Francisco
Santorini
Sardinia
Scotland
Seychelles
Shanghai
Sicily
Singapore
South Africa
Sri Lanka
Stockholm
Switzerland
Tenerife
Thailand
Tokyo
Turkey
Turkey South Coast
Tuscany
United Arab Emirates
USA Southwest (Las Vegas, Colorado, New Mexico, Arizona & Utah)
Venice
Vienna
Vietnam
Zakynthos & Ithaca, Kefalonia, Lefkas

Travel with Insider Tips

INDEX

This index lists all sights, destinations and lakes featured in this guide. Numbers in bold indicate a main entry.

CREDITS

WRITE TO US

e-mail: info@marcopologuides.co.uk
Did you have a great holiday?
Is there something on your mind?
Whatever it is, let us know!
Whether you want to praise, alert us
to errors or give us a personal tip –
MARCO POLO would be pleased to
hear from you.
We do everything we can to provide the
very latest information for your trip.

Nevertheless, despite all of our authors'
thorough research, errors can creep in.
MARCO POLO does not accept any
liability for this. Please contact us by
e-mail or post.
MARCO POLO Travel Publishing Ltd
Pinewood, Chineham Business Park
Crockford Lane, Chineham
Basingstoke, Hampshire RG24 8AL
United Kingdom

PICTURE CREDITS
Cover photograph: Wast Water (Schapowalow: A. Piai)
Photos: Getty Images: N. Bidgood (5, 26/27), Kluboby (19 top), T. Moore (3), J. D. Price (34); Getty Images/Cultura: S. Delauw (18 bottom); Getty Images/Photolibrary: T. Platt (22); Getty Images/Redferns: A. Benge (109); huber-images: A. Piai (88/89), M. Ripani (74/75), R. Taylor (37), C. Warren (60/61), S. Wasek (69, 87); Interfoto: A. Burton (20/21); Interfoto/LatitudeStock: E. Durnford (70); Interfoto/National Trust Photo Library: S. Barber (11); Laif/Loop Images: D. Cheshire (122/123), A. Stowe (14/15); Laif/Redux/VWPics: M. Longhurst (32/33); Laif/robertharding: A. Treadway (4 bottom, 100/101); Look/robertharding (flap right, 110 top); mauritius images: S. Vidler (17, 85), J. Warburton-Lee/M. Sykes (30/31), J. Warburton-Lee/W. Gray (19 bottom); mauritius images/ age fotostock: J. Greenberg (95), C. Joiner (2), S. Wasek (66); mauritius images/Alamy: AndySmyStock (28 right), A. Cooper pics (30), J. Davidson Photos (73, 76/77), K. George (31), T. Graham (107), P. Heinrich (108/109),
J[...]29), M. Longhurst (7), J. Morrison (108), J. Norman
[...]umbria (9), M. Sargent (6), travelbild (93), travelib
[...]ter (10), P. Warren (42), S. Whaley (56), R. Whalley
[...]ges/Foodanddrinkphotos: Foodfolio (28 left); mau-
[...]nages/Loop Images: D. Cheshire (12/13), C. Joiner
[...]nages/robertharding: J. Emmerson (97); mauritius
[...]iance/robertharding: A. Treadway (104/105); Scha-
[...]ages/Loop Images (65, 110 bottom)

[...]ewood, Chineham Business Park, Crockford Lane,
[...]sales@marcopolouk.com © MAIRDUMONT GmbH

[...]er, Tamara Hub, Johanna Jiranek, Nikolai Michaelis,
[...]terer
[...]thfildern
[...]dio für Brand Profiling, Hamburg; design inside:
[...]n Chaaban Dipl.-Des. (FH)

[...] Sabine A. Werner, Mainz: Angela Atkinson, Julia
[...]ons, Mainz, in

[...]d, stored in a
[...]ns (electronic,
[...]t prior written

MIX
Paper from
responsible sources
FSC® C124385

131

DOS & DON'TS ✋

A few things to remember when you are in the Lake District

DO TAKE A MAP

As lovely as the walks and hikes around the Lake District are, the paths are not always well sign-posted, and you could take a wrong turn minutes after you set off. Do not rely on online maps or apps; you'll often find you don't even have any signal in the mountains.

DON'T UNDERESTIMATE THE WEATHER

Always check the weather forecast before setting off on a walk in the mountains. Strong winds, rain or even storms can suddenly occur. Help may be some distance away: mobile phone reception is usually poor to non-existent in the more isolated regions with few inhabitants.

DON'T PARK BADLY

Only park where it is permitted. If you need to take a ticket from a machine, please do so. Even out in the countryside checks are made, and many car parks also have number-plate recognition. Fines are high, and car hire companies will often also charge a tough processing fee.

DO SHOP LOCALLY

If you see a "Farm Shop" sign on your travels, do try to make a stop. By supporting local businesses and shopping locally you will be rewarded with the best and freshest produce the area has to offer.

DON'T ADD ICE TO YOUR WHISKY

Due to its proximity to Scotland, whisky is available all over the Lake District. But you should never add ice to it (or coke). As far as the British are concerned, this ruins it. At most, add a few drops of spring water.

DON'T GO SWIMMING WHEREVER YOU WANT TO

The lakes in the National Park are not for the faint-hearted. The water is cold twelve months of the year, and some of them are very deep. In fact, you're not even allowed to swim in Ennerdale Water, Haweswater and Thirlmere.

DO BOOK IN ADVANCE

Especially in the summer months, the Lake District becomes very busy with holidaymakers. To avoid disappointment, be sure to book your accommodation well in advance. This also goes for restaurants, especially at weekends.